Library of
Davidson College

SCOTTISH CLASSICAL STUDIES

SPARTAN LAW

by
DOUGLAS M. MACDOWELL

SCOTTISH ACADEMIC PRESS
EDINBURGH

Published by
Scottish Academic Press Ltd
33 Montgomery Street, Edinburgh EH7 5JX

ISBN 0 7073 0470 9

© 1986 Douglas M. MacDowell

All rights reserved. No part of this publication may be reproduced, stored in a retrieval system, or transmitted, in any form or by any means, electronic, mechanical, photocopying, recording or otherwise, without the prior permission of Scottish Academic Press Ltd.

British Library Cataloguing in Publication Data

MacDowell, D. M.
 Spartan law.—(Scottish classical studies)
 1. Law—Sparta (Ancient city)
 I. Title II. Series
 343.8'9 [LAW]

ISBN 0 7073 0470 9

Printed in Great Britain by
Clark Constable, Edinburgh and London

Contents

	Preface	vii
	Abbreviations and bibliography	ix
I	Law and legend	1
II	Status	23
III	Military service and the *agoge*	52
IV	Women and marriage	71
V	Landholding and inheritance	89
VI	The austere life	111
VII	The administration of justice	123
VIII	Conclusion	151
	Appendix. The age-groups	159
	Index of passages	168
	Index of Greek words	176
	Index of subjects	178

Preface

Students of ancient Greek law are often warned not to assume that other cities had the same laws as Athens. Yet it is hard to find a coherent account of the legal system of any other city with which Athens may be contrasted. I have therefore tried here to provide such an account. Sparta is the obvious city to choose because of its importance and its opposition to Athens. The difficulties, though, are considerable: the unwritten character of much of Spartan law, the incompleteness of the evidence, and the notorious tendency of later writers to convert Spartan life into a legend. Some of the problems have been strongly disputed in modern times, and I cannot expect everyone to agree with all that I have written, but I hope that even those who disagree will find the collection of evidence useful.

The boundaries of the subject are difficult to define. I have kept mainly to the law as it affected individual Spartans. I have not discussed constitutional law, except incidentally, because a great deal has already been written by others on the Spartan constitution. I omit also sacred law and the organization of the army. I concentrate on the classical period, the fifth and fourth centuries B.C.

The book was completed in the autumn of 1984, and does not take account of any publications which had not reached me by then. At that stage it was read by two friends, Peter Rhodes and Ronald Knox; I am grateful to them for their judicious comments and helpful criticisms, which enabled me to improve it in various ways. I should also like to record here my thanks to Mrs. Betty Gardiner, who has typed not only this book but all my published work during the last ten years.

It is a special privilege for me to inaugurate a series of Scottish Classical Studies. Hitherto work done in Scotland on Greek and Roman subjects has usually had to be published in England or further afield; and I hope that the new series, by bringing together work from the various Scottish universities, will display something of the Scottish contribution to the continuing classical tradition. At a difficult period for academic publishing, much credit is due to the Scottish Academic Press for their willingness to undertake it.

Glasgow D. M. M.

Abbreviations and Bibliography

The abbreviations used for ancient authors and texts will be familiar to most readers of this book. If elucidation is needed, help may be obtained from the lists in Liddell and Scott's *Greek-English Lexicon*, revised by Jones (which I abbreviate to LSJ). But some of my abbreviations are less drastic than theirs, and some are not Latinized. Thus Xenophon's Ἑλληνικά are Xen. *Hell.* (rather than X.*HG*) and Plutarch's Ἠθικά are Plu. *Eth.* (rather than Plu. *Mor.* or 2).

In Plutarch's *Lives*, subsections of chapters are numbered as in the Teubner edition, not the Loeb.

The following list of modern books and articles is not a complete bibliography of Sparta (which would be many times longer), but gives details of works for which I use abbreviated references.

Africa, Thomas W., 'Cleomenes III and the helots', *California Studies in Classical Antiquity* 1 (1968) 1-11.
———, *Phylarchus and the Spartan Revolution*, University of California Publications in History 68 (Berkeley, 1961).
Aly, Wolfgang, *Fragmentum Vaticanum de eligendis magistratibus*, Studi e Testi 104 (Vatican City, 1943).
Asheri, David, 'Laws of inheritance, distribution of land and political constitutions in ancient Greece', *Historia* 12 (1963) 1-21.
———, 'Sulla legge di Epitadeo', *Athenaeum* 39 (1961) 45-68.
Beattie, A. J., 'An early Laconian *lex sacra*', *Classical Quarterly* (new series) 1 (1951) 46-58.

Berthiaume, Guy, 'Citoyens spécialistes à Sparte', *Mnemosyne* (series IV) 29 (1976) 360-4.

Bicknell, P. J., 'Herodotus 9.35.1; or, Could Isagoras have become a Spartan?', *Acta Classica* 25 (1982) 127-30.

Billheimer, Albert, *Τὰ δέκα ἀφ' ἥβης*, *Transactions of the American Philological Association* 77 (1946) 214-20.

——, 'Age-classes in Spartan education', *Transactions of the American Philological Association* 78 (1947) 99-104.

Bockisch, Gabriele, *Ἁρμοσταί*, *Klio* 46 (1965) 129-239.

Boer, W. den, *Laconian Studies* (Amsterdam, 1954).

Bonner, Robert J., and Smith, Gertrude, 'Administration of justice in Sparta', *Classical Philology* 37 (1942) 113-29.

Brelich, Angelo, *Paides e parthenoi* volume 1 (Rome, 1969).

Cartledge, Paul A., 'Did Spartan citizens ever practise a manual *tekhne*?', *Liverpool Classical Monthly* 1 (1976) 115-19.

——, 'The politics of Spartan pederasty', *Proceedings of the Cambridge Philological Society* 207 (1981) 17-36.

——, *Sparta and Lakonia* (London, 1979).

——, 'Spartan wives: liberation or licence?', *Classical Quarterly* (new series) 31 (1981) 84-105.

Cawkwell, G. L., 'Agesilaus and Sparta', *Classical Quarterly* (new series) 26 (1976) 62-84.

——, 'The decline of Sparta', *Classical Quarterly* (new series) 33 (1983) 385-400.

Chrimes, K. M. T., *Ancient Sparta* (Manchester, 1949).

——, *The Respublica Lacedaemoniorum ascribed to Xenophon* (Manchester, 1948).

Christien, Jacqueline, 'La loi d'Épitadeus', *Revue Historique de Droit* 52 (1974) 197-221.

Cozzoli, Umberto, *Proprietà fondiaria ed esercito nello stato spartano dell'età classica* (Rome, 1979).

——, 'Sparta e l'affrancamento degli iloti nel V e nel IV secolo', *Sesta miscellanea greca e romana* (Rome, 1978) 213-32.

Daube, David, 'The duty of procreation', *Proceedings of the Classical Association* 74 (1977) 10-25.

David, Ephraim, *Sparta between Empire and Revolution (404-243 B.C.)* (New York, 1981).

Diller, Aubrey, 'A new source on the Spartan *ephebia*', *American Journal of Philology* 62 (1941) 499-501.

Ducat, Jean, 'Aspects de l'hilotisme', *Ancient Society* 9 (1978) 5-46.

Finley, M. I., 'Sparta', reprinted in his *The Use and Abuse of History* (London, 1975) 161-77, and in his *Economy and Society in Ancient Greece* (London, 1981) 24-40.

Forrest, W. G., *A History of Sparta 950-192 B.C.* (London, 1968).

——, 'Legislation in Sparta', *Phoenix* 21 (1967) 11-19.

Gabba, Emilio, 'Studi su Filarco: le biografie plutarchee di Agide e di Cleomene', *Athenaeum* 35 (1957) 3-55 and 193-239.

Gomme, A. W., *A Historical Commentary on Thucydides* volume 1 (Oxford, 1945).

Hammond, N. G. L., *Studies in Greek History* (Oxford, 1973).

Higgins, W. E., *Xenophon the Athenian* (Albany, 1977).

Hodkinson, Stephen, 'Social order and the conflict of values in classical Sparta', *Chiron* 13 (1983) 239-81.

Jacoby, Felix, *Die Fragmente der griechischen Historiker* (Berlin and Leiden, 1923-58).

Jones, A. H. M., *Sparta* (Oxford, 1967).

Kahrstedt, Ulrich, *Griechisches Staatsrecht, Erster Band: Sparta und seine Symmachie* (Göttingen, 1922).

Karabélias, E., 'L'épiclérat à Sparte', *Studi in onore di Arnaldo Biscardi* (Milan, 1982) 2.469-80.

Keaney, John J., 'Theophrastus on Greek judicial procedure', *Transactions of the American Philological Association* 104 (1974) 179-94.

Kiechle, Franz, *Lakonien und Sparta* (Munich, 1963).
Lacey, W. K., *The Family in Classical Greece* (London, 1968).
Lewis, David M., *Sparta and Persia* (Leiden, 1977).
Lotze, Detlef, Μεταξὺ ἐλευθέρων καὶ δούλων, *Studien zur Rechtsstellung unfreier Landbevölkerungen in Griechenland bis zum 4. Jahrhundert v. Chr.*, Deutsche Akademie der Wissenschaften zu Berlin, Schriften der Sektion für Altertumswissenschaft 17 (1959).
——, Μόθακες, *Historia* 11 (1962) 427-35.
Marasco, Gabriele, 'Aristotele come fonte di Plutarco nelle biografie di Agide e Cleomene', *Athenaeum* 56 (1978) 170-181.
——, 'La leggenda di Polidoro e la ridistribuzione di terre di Licurgo nella propaganda spartana del III secolo', *Prometheus* 4 (1978) 115-27.
Marrou, H.-I., 'Les classes d'âge de la jeunesse spartiate', *Revue des Etudes Anciennes* 48 (1946) 216-30.
Mendels, Doron, 'Sparta in Teles' περὶ φυγῆς', *Eranos* 77 (1979) 111-15.
Michell, H., *Sparta* (Cambridge, 1952).
Momigliano, Arnaldo, 'Per l'unità logica della Λακεδαιμονίων πολιτεία di Senofonte', *Rivista di Filologia e d'Istruzione Classica* (nuova serie) 14 (1936) 170-3.
Oliva, Pavel, *Sparta and her Social Problems* (Amsterdam and Prague, 1971).
Ollier, François, *Le Mirage spartiate* volumes 1 and 2 (Paris, 1933-43).
——, *Xénophon: La République des Lacédémoniens* (Lyon, 1934).
Ostwald, Martin, *Nomos and the Beginnings of the Athenian Democracy* (Oxford, 1969).
Parke, H. W., 'The evidence for harmosts in Laconia', *Hermathena* 46 (1931) 31-8.
Quass, Friedemann, *Nomos und Psephisma* (Munich, 1971).

Rhodes, P. J., 'The selection of ephors at Sparta', *Historia* 30 (1981) 498-502.

Richards, Herbert, *Notes on Xenophon and Others* (London, 1907).

Roussel, P., 'L'exposition des enfants à Sparte', *Revue des Études Anciennes* 45 (1943) 5-17.

Ste. Croix, G. E. M. de, *The Origins of the Peloponnesian War* (London, 1972).

Schaps, David M., *Economic Rights of Women in Ancient Greece* (Edinburgh, 1979).

Tazelaar, C. M., 'Παῖδες καὶ ἔφηβοι: some notes on the Spartan stages of youth', *Mnemosyne* (series IV) 20 (1967) 127-53.

Tigerstedt, E. N., *The Legend of Sparta in Classical Antiquity* volumes 1-3 (Stockholm and Uppsala, 1965-78).

Tonini, Teresa Alfieri, 'Il problema dei "neodamodeis" nell'ambito della società spartana', *Rendiconti dell'Istituto Lombardo, Classe di Lettere* 109 (1975) 305-16.

Toynbee, Arnold, *Some Problems of Greek History* (London, 1969).

Wade-Gery, H. T., *Essays in Greek History* (Oxford, 1958).

Walbank, F. W., *A Historical Commentary on Polybius* volume 1 (Oxford, 1957).

Welwei, Karl-Wilhelm, *Unfreie im antiken Kriegsdienst, Erster Teil: Athen und Sparta* (Wiesbaden, 1974).

Westlake, H. D., 'Reelection to the ephorate?', *Greek, Roman and Byzantine Studies* 17 (1976) 343-52.

——, 'Thucydides on Pausanias and Themistocles — a written source?', *Classical Quarterly* (new series) 27 (1977) 95-110.

Willetts, R. F., 'The neodamodeis', *Classical Philology* 49 (1954) 27-32.

Wüst, Fritz R., 'Laconica', *Klio* 37 (1959) 53-62.

I

Law and Legend

THE LAWS OF LYKOURGOS

Sparta in the fifth and fourth centuries B.C. was notorious for its unique constitution and austere way of life, especially its manner of rearing boys and making them into soldiers. The rules of the system are generally called 'the νόμοι of Lykourgos'. The word νόμος may be translated 'law', though it has a wider sense than that English word. It includes customs and practices which must be observed or ought to be observed, even if not laid down by statute or enforced by public authority. However, it is not necessary here to investigate the full range of the word's meaning. It is clear that, when Spartan νόμοι are attributed to Lykourgos, what is meant is that Lykourgos formulated rules and, whatever exactly was the basis of his authority (he is said by Hdt. 1.65.4 to have been the guardian of king Leobotas, his nephew, whereas according to Plu. *Lyk.* 5.6 he obtained power by a show of force), required the Spartans to obey them: ἐφύλαξε ταῦτα μὴ παραβαίνειν, 'he made sure that they did not transgress these' (Hdt. 1.65.5). This is near enough to the modern concept of law, and so we may call these νόμοι 'laws'. (Fuller examination of the concept of νόμος may be found in the books on that subject by Ostwald and Quass.)

Whether these laws were really made by Lykourgos is doubtful. His date is quite uncertain. Herodotos is all but self-contradictory: he writes as if Lykourgos had lived not long before kings Leon and Agesikles at the beginning of the sixth century (1.65.1, cf. 1.66.1), and yet the association of him with king Leobotas, who was the ancestor of king Leonidas in the twelfth generation, seems to imply a date in the ninth century (1.65.4, cf. 7.204). The latter is consistent with Thucydides, who, according to the better interpretation of a difficult sentence, dates the establishment of a law-abiding society in Sparta a little more than four hundred years before the end of the Peloponnesian War (1.18.1; cf. Ostwald *Nomos* 79-80). An alternative tradition placed Lykourgos even earlier, at the time when a Dorian state was first established at Sparta; at least, that may be what Xenophon means by saying that he lived at the time of the Herakleidai (*LP* 10.8), and Hellanikos also attributed the laws to a similar period when, without mentioning Lykourgos, he said that Eurysthenes and Prokles, the first kings of Sparta, organized the state (*F. Gr. Hist.* 4 F116, from Strabo 8.5.5). Aristotle, however, found what he considered good evidence that Lykourgos lived at the time of the first Olympic festival in 776 (fr. 533); this and other views are recorded in Plu. *Lyk.* 1. Modern historians are as far from a consensus as ancient ones. They have adduced archaeological evidence, but are not agreed about the relevance of that evidence to the constitution and legal system. Some have maintained that Lykourgos was a mythical figure who never really existed, and the dates favoured for the legislation attributed to him range from the ninth century to the sixth.

I have nothing to say about that problem, and my concern in this book is a different one, the elucidation of the Spartan legal system as it existed in the fifth and fourth centuries. Whether Lykourgos ever existed or not, there is no doubt that 'the laws of Lykourgos' did exist, because that was the name given to the system which was in use in the fifth century. We may compare 'the laws of Solon', which was the name given to the Athenian system at the same period. Solon was certainly a historical figure, but it is known that not all 'the laws of Solon' were actually made by him; for example, Andokides calls the decree of Demophantos, which is shown by its prescript to have been made in 410, τὸν Σόλωνος νόμον (1.95-6). So it is possible that in Sparta likewise Lykourgos really did make some laws, but that other laws attributed to him were added by other people at later dates. That does not affect their authenticity as laws of the classical system.

It was believed that Lykourgos obtained his laws from the Delphic oracle, or at least got the oracle's approval before they were put into effect (Hdt. 1.65.2-4, Xen. *LP* 8.5). Plutarch says that it was because they were the god's pronouncements that they were called ῥῆτραι (*Lyk*. 13.11). Etymologically ῥήτρα just means 'saying', and there is no other evidence that it means a divine saying in particular. Even if that was its sense at one time, it certainly came to be used of laws which had no such origin, and thus was just a synonym for νόμος (Xen. *An*. 6.6.28, Plu. *Agis* 5.3, 8.1, etc.; cf. Wade-Gery *Essays* 62-5, Quass *Nomos* 7-9).

Were these ῥῆτραι written? Plutarch says that Lykourgos did not put his laws in writing (*Lyk*. 13.1, *Eth*. 227b), and yet he quotes the text of one of them, on the subject of decision-making by the kings, elders, and people.

Plu. *Lyk*. 6.1-2, 7-8. οὕτω δὲ περὶ ταύτην ἐσπούδασε τὴν ἀρχὴν ὁ Λυκοῦργος, ὥστε μαντείαν ἐκ Δελφῶν κομίσαι περὶ αὐτῆς, ἣν ῥήτραν καλοῦσιν. ἔχει δ' οὕτως· "Διὸς Σκυλλανίου καὶ Ἀθανᾶς Σκυλλανίας ἱερὸν ἱδρυσάμενον, φυλὰς φυλάξαντα καὶ ὠβὰς ὠβάξαντα τριάκοντα γερουσίαν σὺν ἀρχαγέταις καταστήσαντα ὥραις ἐξ ὡρᾶν ἀπελλάζειν μεταξὺ Βαβύκας τε καὶ

Κνακιῶνος, οὕτως εἰσφέρειν τε καὶ ἀφίστασθαι· †γαμω-δανγοριανημην καὶ κράτος." ... ὕστερον μέντοι τῶν πολλῶν ἀφαιρέσει καὶ προσθέσει τὰς γνώμας διαστρεφόντων καὶ παραβιαζομένων, Πολύδωρος καὶ Θεόπομπος οἱ βασιλεῖς τάδε τῇ ῥήτρᾳ παρενέγραψαν· "αἰ δὲ σκολιὰν ὁ δᾶμος αἱροῖτο, τοὺς πρεσβυγενέας καὶ ἀρχαγέτας ἀποστατῆρας ἦμεν." (The text given here is that of Ziegler's Teubner edition. Many details are disputed, and the translation which follows is only approximate.) 'Lykourgos attached such importance to this office that he brought an oracle from Delphi about it, which they call a rhetra. It is as follows. "After establishing a temple of Zeus Skyllanios and Athena Skyllania, after organizing tribes and obes, and after setting up a senate of thirty men with the leaders, from season to season there are to be *apellai* between Babyka and Knakion, and thus there is to be introduction and dispatch; [text corrupt]." ... But later, when the people by subtraction and addition distorted and perverted the proposals, kings Polydoros and Theopompos wrote in this rider to the rhetra. "But if the people should make a crooked choice, the elders and leaders are to be dispatchers."'

Despite textual difficulties, it seems clear that the language of this rhetra and its rider is archaic and Doric, and that it is a genuine early Spartan document. Nearly all modern scholars accept it as such, and discuss it as 'the Great Rhetra' (Wade-Gery *Essays* 37-85, Hammond *Studies* 47-103, Forrest *Sparta* 40-60, Oliva *Sparta* 71-102, and many others). Plutarch says that Polydoros and Theopompos 'wrote in' the rider, and he goes on (in *Lyk*. 6.9-10) to quote a poem of Tyrtaios (fr. 4 West) which refers to the law with the rider. Thus it appears

LAW AND LEGEND

that at least one of 'the laws of Lykourgos' was in writing by the time of Tyrtaios, before the end of the seventh century. Later laws were certainly written: the phrase ῥήτραν γράφειν is used to mean 'propose a law' (Plu. *Agis* 5.3, 9.1), and in the fourth century the Athenian orator Lykourgos was able to have the text of a Spartan law read out in an Athenian court (*Leo.* 129). But no stone inscriptions of laws of the classical period have been found at Sparta, and we hear nothing of any attempt to make a comprehensive written code, such as occurred at Athens at the end of the fifth century. It is likely that many of 'the laws of Lykourgos' remained unwritten.

SUBSEQUENT LEGISLATION

Plutarch says that the laws of Lykourgos remained unaltered for five hundred years; but even he concedes that additions were made to them, and after the late fifth century there were other changes (*Lyk.* 29.10-11). By what procedure were new laws made and old ones repealed or amended? The rhetra attributed to Lykourgos lays down a legislative procedure, but even if we could interpret the details of that early document confidently, we could not be confident that the same procedure was still followed in the fifth and fourth centuries. For that period, the only information about the procedure comes from Plutarch's accounts of three pieces of legislation: a law forbidding the import of gold and silver currency, made soon after the end of the Peloponnesian War (*Lys.* 17.2-6); a law about landholding, proposed by Epitadeus, probably in the latter part of the fifth century (*Agis* 5.3-4; on the date see pages 104-5); and a law about cancellation of debts and redistribution of land, proposed in the reign of Agis IV (*Agis* 8-11). The last falls outside our period, but may be used as evidence here because of the probability that Agis, who claimed to be a champion of tradition, upheld the traditional procedure.

From this evidence it appears that the procedure had three stages. First, the proposal was put in writing and brought forward by one or more of the ephors. The ephors' role is clear in all three instances.

> Plu. *Lys.* 17.2. οἱ δὲ φρονιμώτατοι τῶν Σπαρτιατῶν ... διεμαρτύραντο τοῖς ἐφόροις ἀποδιοπομπεῖσθαι πᾶν τὸ ἀργύριον καὶ τὸ χρυσίον ὥσπερ κῆρας ἐπαγωγίμους. οἱ δὲ προύθεσαν γνώμην. 'The most sensible of the Spartiates ... called on the ephors to banish all the silver and gold as imported blights. And they (the ephors) put forward a proposal.'

> Plu. *Agis* 5.3. ἐφορεύσας δέ τις ἀνὴρ δυνατός, αὐθάδης δὲ καὶ χαλεπὸς τὸν τρόπον, Ἐπιτάδευς ὄνομα, ... ῥήτραν ἔγραψεν. 'But when a certain powerful man became an ephor, a man wilful and difficult in character, named Epitadeus, ... he proposed a rhetra.'

> Plu. *Agis* 8.1. οὐ μὴν ἀλλὰ διαπραξάμενος ὁ Ἆγις ἔφορον γενέσθαι τὸν Λύσανδρον, εὐθὺς εἰσέφερε δι' αὐτοῦ ῥήτραν εἰς τοὺς γέροντας. 'Nevertheless Agis, after contriving that Lysander became an ephor, immediately introduced a rhetra through him to the senators.'

It is noticeable that 'the most sensible of the Spartiates' could not propose a law themselves, but had to get the ephors to do it; Epitadeus, though a powerful man, could not propose a law until he became an ephor; and Agis, though a king, got his friend to become an ephor to propose a law for him. So it appears that only an ephor could propose a law.

The second stage was the senate. This is not mentioned in the first two instances, but it is clear in the third. Lysander introduced Agis's rhetra to the senate (Plu. *Agis* 8.1); the senators did not all agree (9.1); the matter was debated in the assembly of citizens (9-10), and then:

> Plu. *Agis* 11.1. ἐκ τούτου τῷ μὲν Ἄγιδι τὸ πλῆθος ἐπηκολούθησεν, οἱ δὲ πλούσιοι τόν τε Λεωνίδαν παρεκάλουν μὴ σφᾶς προέσθαι, καὶ τοὺς γέροντας, οἷς τὸ κράτος ἦν ἐν τῷ προβουλεύειν, δεόμενοι καὶ πείθοντες ἴσχυσαν, ὅσον ἑνὶ πλείονας γενέσθαι τοὺς ἀποψηφισαμένους τὴν ῥήτραν. 'As a result of this the people agreed with Agis. But the rich men called on Leonidas not to abandon them, and by entreating and urging the senators, whose power lay in preliminary deliberation, they prevailed, to the extent that those voting against the rhetra had a majority of one.'

The meaning of προβουλεύειν in constitutional contexts is well known: it refers to a council's power to decide whether a proposal is to be placed before a larger assembly. So this passage shows that the Spartan senate had power to decide whether a proposed law should be passed to the assembly of citizens. In this particular case they decided that it should not, and that was legally the end of the matter. But if the majority of senators had voted in favour of the law, it would still have had to be voted on by the assembly of citizens afterwards. That, the third stage of the procedure, is implied by the prefix προ- in προβουλεύειν, which shows that the decision by the assembly had to be preceded by the senate's decision. Thus we may not say that the assembly's decision had already been made at the meeting described in *Agis* 9-10. Why then was that earlier meeting of the assembly held? Forrest *Phoenix* 21 (1967) 11-19 has argued from this instance (and from Diod. 11.50, where the matter under consideration is not legislation but a declaration of war) that the procedure required four meetings in the order senate, assembly, senate, assembly; the first meeting of each body merely discussed, the second decided. No evidence refutes that hypothesis, but it remains uncertain; if the senate and the assembly sometimes considered a proposal at more than one meeting, that does not prove that they had to do so in every instance. To be cautious, it is better just to say that the three necessary stages for legislation were that the proposal should be initiated by an ephor, passed by the senate, and finally ratified by the assembly. That made it a valid law.

XENOPHON'S *LAKEDAIMONION POLITEIA*
  The earliest surviving attempt to give a comprehensive account of the laws of Lykourgos is Xenophon's *Lakedaimonion Politeia* (which I call *LP* for short). Its composition and date have been much discussed; for a full (though not complete) bibliography see Tigerstedt *Legend* 1.455-64, especially note 530. Some scholars (including Chrimes *Resp. Lac.*, Wüst *Klio* 37 (1959) 53-60) have suggested that it was not written by Xenophon, but Richards *Xenophon* 40-47 shows that Xenophon is certainly the author; the evidence of vocabulary and style is overwhelming. Xenophon is well known to have been an admirer of Sparta, and especially of king Agesilaos; it was for this reason that he was exiled from Athens and was granted by the Spartans a house and estate at Skillous, near Elis (Diog. Laert. 2.51-2). It is therefore not surprising that he should have written a book explaining his reasons for admiring Sparta, and a recent suggestion that it is ironic (Higgins *Xenophon* 65-75) is certainly wrong. But its arrangement has some puzzling features.
  Most of it praises the laws of Lykourgos as the cause of Sparta's rise to greatness, and describes the institutions and customs resulting from them. Then chapter 14 says 'If

anyone were to ask me if the laws of Lykourgos seemed to me to remain still unchanged even now, I really would no longer assert that with confidence', and proceeds to give several examples of ways in which the laws of Lykourgos are no longer upheld. But chapters 1-13 give no hint that the laws are not still observed, and in several places imply that they are. Whereas the actions of Lykourgos are in the past (denoted by aorist verbs), practices resulting from his laws are mentioned in the present tense (4.3-6, 6.2-3, 6.5, etc.), and 'you' (second person singular) can observe the effect on the young men of their strict upbringing (3.5). The most striking contrast is between 7.6, which says that any Spartan found to possess gold and silver is punished, and 14.3, which says that now some Spartans pride themselves on possessing gold. Most modern readers have concluded that chapter 14 is a postscript, written at a later date than the rest.

That conclusion is rejected by some (including Momigliano *RIFC* 14 (1936) 170-3, Chrimes *Resp. Lac.* 1-8, Higgins *Xenophon* 66). It may be conceded that 14.1 does not mean that all the laws of Lykourgos, but only that some of them, are no longer observed; so this statement is not in direct contradiction with statements that particular laws are still in force. But the contradiction between 7.6 and 14.3 cannot be evaded in this way, because they both refer to the same law; Chrimes's attempt to argue that the present tense in 7.6 refers to the idealized Sparta of Lykourgos, whereas the present tense in 14.3 refers to the time of Xenophon, is not satisfactory. Equally unsatisfactory is Momigliano's interpretation of 1.1 as meaning that the laws of Lykourgos were in force when Xenophon studied them but not when he wrote *LP* (implying a longer interval between research and writing than even modern scholars usually perpetrate). 1.1 says κατενόησα τὰ ἐπιτηδεύματα τῶν Σπαρτιατῶν, 'I studied the practices of the Spartans', not 'the former practices', and it would be very strange for Xenophon to conceal so completely throughout chapters 1-13 that the practices described belonged to the past and not to the present, if he already had it in mind to make that point in chapter 14. We should therefore adhere to the usual view that chapter 14 is a postscript, added after his estimation of the Spartans had fallen for some reason.

But if chapter 14 is a postscript, why is it not at the end of the book? Perhaps that is indeed where it ought to be; thus Ollier, in his edition of *LP*, transposes and renumbers chapters 14 and 15. At first sight it seems convincing that the two chapters (13 and 15) which deal with the duties and privileges of kings should be consecutive. Palaeographical explanations of the misplacing of chapter 14 have been suggested: the last leaf of a codex, having chapter 15 on one side and 14 on the other, may have got turned back to front, or the postscript (chapter 14) may have been originally written in the margin of the last page of the book (cf. Chrimes *Resp. Lac.* 3). Some such explanation may be right, but another explanation, I suggest, is possible: chapter 15 may be a second postscript, added later than chapter 14. For in 11.1 Xenophon says that he has completed his account of good institutions common to peace and war, and will now go on to the organization of military expeditions. Chapters 11-13 are duly devoted to military practices, but then 15.1 begins: 'I also want to relate the arrangements which Lykourgos made between a king and the city'. The rest of chapter 15, though it mentions the king's command of the army at one point (15.2), is mostly about the life of a king at home in Sparta. Thus it belongs logically to the account of institutions in Sparta (chapters 1-10) rather than to the account of campaigns abroad (chapters 11-13), and its position at the end of the book is most easily explained by the hypothesis that it is a later addition, written perhaps after Xenophon had had an opportunity to observe more fully how the kings lived when they were at home.

Now for the evidence of the date: chapter 14 contains two indications of the period when it was written. First there are the references to Spartans who govern (ἁρμόζειν) in foreign cities (14.2 and 14.4). Spartan harmosts overseas existed at least as early as 412 (Thuc. 8.5.2) and still existed in the 370s, but were probably most numerous between the Peloponnesian War and the King's Peace (404-386). Secondly, a contrast is drawn in 14.6 between the old days and the present.

> Xen. *LP* 14.6. οἱ Ἕλληνες πρότερον μὲν ἰόντες εἰς Λακεδαίμονα ἐδέοντο αὐτῶν ἡγεῖσθαι ἐπὶ τοὺς δοκοῦντας ἀδικεῖν· νῦν δὲ πολλοὶ παρακαλοῦσιν ἀλλήλους ἐπὶ τὸ διακωλύειν ἄρξαι πάλιν αὐτούς. 'The Greeks previously used to go to Lakedaimon and ask them (the Spartans) to take the lead against those considered to be offenders; but now many call on one another to stop them ruling again.'

The first half of this sentence refers to a period which the author regards as long past, possibly the Persian Wars, but more probably the events leading to the outbreak of the Peloponnesian War (the alleged offenders being the Athenians). The second half refers to the present time, but scholars' efforts to identify it have revealed an ambiguity in the word πάλιν. This word can mean either 'back', 'contrariwise' (LSJ s.v. I.2) or 'for a second time', 'once more' (LSJ s.v. II). If we take it in the former sense, it goes with διακωλύειν, and the sentence was written at a time when the Spartans held the hegemony of Greece and other Greeks were trying to depose them from it. If we take it in the latter sense, it goes with ἄρξαι, and the sentence was written at a time when the Spartans did not hold the hegemony and other Greeks were trying to prevent them from regaining it. The contrast with the first half of the sentence favours the former interpretation, and the aorist aspect of ἄρξαι favours the latter, but neither of these considerations is decisive. Although some scholars have insisted on one interpretation and some on the other, we must accept that πάλιν is ambiguous here and no conclusion may be founded upon it.

Nor does there seem to be any other way of pinning this sentence to an exact date. The reference to other Greeks combining against Sparta has made some scholars think of the alliance leading to the Corinthian War in 395/4 (cf. Cawkwell *CQ* 33 (1983) 395 n.38), others of the formation of the Second Athenian Confederacy in 378/7 (cf. Ollier's edition of *LP* pp. xiv-xv). But νῦν cannot be pressed to mean 'in this very year'; it just means 'nowadays', by contrast with forty or more years ago, and there was perhaps hardly any time between 400 and 371 when it could not have been said that many Greeks wanted to stop the Spartans from either continuing or regaining their hegemony.

Attempts to date *LP* as a whole have also had little success. W. Dittenberger *Hermes* 16 (1881) 332 regards it as one of Xenophon's latest works because the particle μήν is relatively frequent in it, but the work is really too short for statistical study of one particle to produce reliable results. E. Delebecque *Essai sur la vie de Xénophon* (1957) 195-6 tries to narrow the range of possible dates by detecting passages in which *LP* replies to works by Plato and Isokrates; but this too is unconvincing, because nothing in *LP* is so worded as to show that it is a reply to a specific work.

What it would be most interesting to know is the cause of

LAW AND LEGEND

Xenophon's disillusionment with Sparta, expressed in chapter 14. It cannot have been the defeat at Leuktra (as suggested by Jacoby *F. Gr. Hist.* IIIb Noten 359 n.25), because the references to harmosts (14.2, 14.4) and to proposals for alliance against Sparta (14.6) were clearly written before then. It may be better to relate his disillusionment to an event in his own life, the occasion when he first saw Sparta for himself. In the 390s he spent some time serving under king Agesilaos in Asia; in 394 he returned to Greece and, being exiled from Athens, went to the Peloponnese and took up residence in Spartan-controlled territory. From what is known of his life, it is improbable that he had any opportunity to visit Sparta before 394. We can suppose that during the campaign in Asia he conceived an admiration for his Spartan colleagues, observed their conduct and discipline, asked them for an account of their upbringing and way of life, and wrote it down for the edification of Athenian and other readers. All this could easily have been done during his leisure hours over a period of a year or more. *LP* 1-10 may even be based on a description of Sparta given to Xenophon by Agesilaos himself; Agesilaos was a staunch upholder of traditional practices, and would have described them in the most favourable way. When Xenophon went to Sparta a year or two later, he would have found that the picture which had been painted for him was too rosy, and that many Spartans did not live quite as Agesilaos said they did; and that would have been the occasion for adding chapter 14.

This explanation of the book's origin is only a possibility, not a certainty; but it does have the merit of accounting for the different tone of chapter 14. If it is something like the truth, we can regard *LP* as good, but not unimpeachable, evidence for Sparta in Xenophon's time. The account of military practice (chapters 11-13) is probably based on his own observation in Asia. A phrase in 13.5, 'If you saw these activities you would think...', probably implies that Xenophon had in fact seen what he describes. Chapter 15, if it is a postscript, may be based on his own observation of the life of Agesilaos in Sparta. But chapters 1-10 may be what the Spartans in Asia told him, rather than what he saw for himself. References to Sparta as ἐκεῖ, 'there' (7.6, 9.6), imply that he was not in Sparta when he was writing. The Spartans in Asia were, of course, an authoritative source of information. But some of what they told him may have been the theory rather than the practice of the Spartan system, the rules rather than the infringements of them. If so, that makes *LP* defective evidence for Spartan life, but still good evidence for Spartan law.

PLUTARCH AND THE SPARTAN LEGEND

The discrepancy between law and practice of which Xenophon complains in *LP* 14 was a recent development. Until the late fifth century there is no reason to think that 'the laws of Lykourgos' were not observed. For Herodotos, writing in the third quarter of that century, they are τὸν νῦν κατεστεῶτα κόσμον Σπαρτιήτῃσι, 'the system now established for the Spartans' (1.65.4). He plainly believes what he makes Demaratos say to Xerxes: law is the Lakedaimonians' master, and implicit obedience to it has made them the best soldiers in the world (7.104.4-5). This is not myth but fact. The Spartans were seen to be the best soldiers at Thermopylai, Plataia, and other battles. Herodotos visited Sparta himself, and would certainly have noticed if 'the laws of Lykourgos' were ceasing to be observed. Thucydides too spent time with the Peloponnesians in the last quarter of the century (5.26.5), and he remarks on the Lakedaimonians' obedience to law and continuation of the same constitution

LAW AND LEGEND

down to the end of the Peloponnesian War (1.18.1). These authors are eyewitnesses, and their statements may not be dismissed as merely a legend about Sparta.

Yet a legend did grow up. It has been studied at great length, though not quite satisfactorily, in two books, Ollier's *Le Mirage spartiate* and Tigerstedt's *The Legend of Sparta in Classical Antiquity*. (Rawson's *The Spartan Tradition in European Thought* is more concerned with later times.) It spread among the long-haired youth of Athens who associated with Sokrates (cf. Ar. *Birds* 1281-2: ἐλακωνομάνουν ... ἐσωκράτων). The attraction of Sparta for Athenian intellectuals in the late fifth century was much like the attraction of Russia for Western intellectuals in the 1930s. It appeared to be morally superior, because its principle was that service to the community was to be given preference over individual pleasure or profit. Besides, they knew that their government and their parents disapproved of it; and since most of them never visited Sparta (unlike Herodotos, Thucydides, and Xenophon), they were not generally disturbed by the sight of facts which did not accord with their idealized view.

One member of this circle in Athens was Kritias, the tyrannical leader of the Thirty in 404/3. He wrote a *Lakedaimonion Politeia*, the first book ever written on that subject as far as is known. It is not known whether he ever visited Sparta. But for the present purpose it is hardly necessary to decide how accurate the book was, because the few surviving fragments are mostly on domestic topics and contain nothing of legal interest (Diels-Kranz 88 B32-7). In one fragment Kritias declares that he is starting with the birth of children (B32), and since Xenophon also starts with that topic (*LP* 1.3) it has been suggested that Xenophon based his work on Kritias's (cf. Tigerstedt *Legend* 1.163 with n.495). But that is very unlikely; the birth and upbringing of children is the most obvious starting-point for anyone's account of the peculiar features of Spartan society, and there is no evidence that Xenophon's book resembled Kritias's in any other way. Xenophon is far more likely to have got his information from the Spartans themselves than from an Athenian book.

Others also wrote in praise of the Spartan constitution (Arist. *Pol.* 1333b 11-21), and by the time Plato wrote his *Republic* and *Laws* he could take the 'Cretan and Lakonic' constitution to be the kind most generally admired (e.g. *Rep.* 544c). Plato's own purpose in both those works is not to praise Sparta but to show how an even better system may be devised; nevertheless the implication is that Spartan and Cretan laws are the best of those devised hitherto. It does not seem to have occurred to him that the Spartans no longer observed their traditional laws, or if it did, he did not care; his interest was theoretical. By this time the philosophers' and moralists' ideal Sparta was fully fledged, and took flight independently of the facts.

But one philosopher was not carried away by it. Aristotle in his *Politics* (especially 1269a 29-1271b 19) makes a series of criticisms of the Spartan constitution and laws, including the organization of the helots, the lax control of women, the role of the ephors, and the laws about property and inheritance. He not only says that some of the laws are bad, but is also aware that some of them are not obeyed in practice. He even knows of specific cases: some ephors were venal because of their poverty, 'and they have shown this on many previous occasions, and also recently in the case of the Andrians; for certain of them, corrupted by money, destroyed the whole city, as far as it lay in their power to do so' (1270b 11-13). This is not legend, but historical information. It is doubtful whether Aristotle ever visited Sparta himself; but if he did and that Plutarch uncritically reproduced it in his double biography of Agis and Kleomenes, and perhaps in his other biographies of Spartans too (cf. Tigerstedt *Legend* 2.76-85).

But that is not a satisfactory line of argument. First, there is no evidence that Phylarkhos wrote about Spartan legislation. He is said to have been a writer who was excessively devoted to producing effects of tragedy and pathos (Polyb. 2.56, Plu. *Them.* 32.4), but law is not a subject which lends itself to such effects. Plutarch in his *Agis and Kleomenes* actually names him as a source only in connection with scenes of treachery (*Kleom.* 5.3, 28.2), death (*Kleom.* 30.3), or myth (*Agis* 9.3). Secondly, the notion that Plutarch followed Phylarkhos exclusively and uncritically is not in accord with what we have already seen of his methods. Some recent historians have treated *Agis and Kleomenes* virtually as if it were the unaltered work of Phylarkhos; this is a serious weakness of Africa's *Phylarchus and the Spartan Revolution*, for example. This error might have been avoided if closer attention had been paid to the manner in which Plutarch from time to time considers alternative views. For instance, with regard to the death of Arkhidamos, brother of Agis: 'they killed him immediately, either against the will of Kleomenes, as Phylarkhos thinks, or because he was persuaded by his friends and gave the man up to them; for most of the blame fell upon them, because they were thought to have constrained Kleomenes' (*Kleom.* 5.3-4). Clearest of all is a passage in which Plutarch quotes Polybios about Aratos and Kleomenes, and then goes on:

> Plu. *Arat.* 38.12. ὁμοίως δὲ καὶ Φύλαρχος ἱστόρηκε περὶ τούτων, ᾧ μὴ τοῦ Πολυβίου μαρτυροῦντος οὐ πάνυ τι πιστεύειν ἄξιον ἦν· ἐνθουσιᾷ γὰρ ὅταν ἅψηται τοῦ Κλεομένους ὑπ' εὐνοίας, καὶ καθάπερ ἐν δίκῃ τῇ ἱστορίᾳ

still preserved in our own time' (*Lyk*. 21.4). He visited Sparta himself (*Lyk*. 18.2), and while he was there he did some research 'in the Lakonian records' (*Ages*. 19.10: ἐν ταῖς Λακωνικαῖς ἀναγραφαῖς), in which he discovered the names of the wife and daughters of Agesilaos. He does not say what the records contained besides genealogies, but one would expect them to have held the texts of those laws which were written down. Perhaps it was there that he found the text of 'the Great Rhetra' (*Lyk*. 6), which he has clearly copied out verbatim, not quoted from memory. An alternative possibility is that he got it from Aristotle, to whom he refers in the course of his interpretation of it. But if we prefer that explanation, then we must concede that he had Aristotle's *LP* open before him as he wrote; and in that case we can be all the more confident that he reproduced accurately the other information which that book contained.

On the whole, therefore, it appears that Plutarch had good sources at his disposal for Sparta of the fifth and fourth centuries, and there is no reason to think that he misused them. However, one possible cause of distortion has still to be considered. In the second half of the third century, by which time many of 'the laws of Lykourgos' were obsolete or widely ignored, kings Agis IV and Kleomenes III each in turn tried to revive them (Plu. *Agis* 4.2, *Kleom*. 10, etc.). The history of that period was written by Phylarkhos (*F. Gr. Hist.* 81). His work is now lost, but he is said to have been very favourable to Kleomenes (Plu. *Arat*. 38.12). It has been suggested that Agis and Kleomenes, or the philosopher Sphairos on their behalf (cf. Ollier *Mirage* 2.99-123), attributed to Lykourgos the measures which they themselves wanted to introduce, in order to make them seem less innovatory and more acceptable; that Phylarkhos incorporated this picture of 'the laws of Lykourgos' into his history;

He refers to about twenty-five different authorities by name in *Lykourgos*. Some modern historians have thought that he just took all these names from some earlier compilation, without reading the various books himself; but that view is now generally and rightly rejected. A much better picture of Plutarch's methods is given by Gomme *HCT* 1.54-84 and F. J. Frost *Plutarch's Themistocles* (1980) 40-59. He was a cultivated and learned man, who read all the principal classical and Hellenistic authors and collected from them the material which was relevant to his *Lives*. Where he has found discrepancies, he records them and sometimes tries to decide which account is more likely to be right. Where he has found no discrepancy and sees no reason for doubt, he generally just asserts a fact without giving his authority. The authors named in *Lykourgos* include some still extant, such as Thucydides, Xenophon, and Plato, and some of whom we know little or nothing, such as Dieutykhidas or Dieukhidas (1.8) and Apollothemis (31.7). He quotes poems of Tyrtaios, Terpander, Pindar, and Alkman (6.10, 21.5-6). But the authority whom he names more often than any other, in this book, is Aristotle. He does not name the work of Aristotle which he is using, but it must surely be the *Lakedaimonion Politeia*. Although there can be no certainty, the probability is that a large proportion of the statements in Plutarch's *Lykourgos* which are made without any named authority are based on Aristotle's *LP*.

That was a good authority for the law of the fifth and fourth centuries. Furthermore, there is no reason to think that Plutarch would have used it carelessly or inaccurately. Even Gomme *HCT* 1.84 is rather too sceptical in asserting that Plutarch was not a researcher and wrote mainly from memory. His quotations from Spartan poems, authentic documents of the archaic age, came from texts which 'were

LAW AND LEGEND

not, he evidently got information from someone who did.

There must have been much more information in the lost *Lakedaimonion Politeia* which was among the 158 accounts of constitutions attributed to Aristotle. A few fragments of it survive (nos. 532-45 in Rose's Teubner edition of the fragments of Aristotle). If it was similar to the extant *Athenaion Politeia*, it consisted of a historical account of the development of Sparta, followed by a fairly comprehensive description of the working of the Spartan state in his own time. The *Athenaion Politeia* is criticized by modern scholars for inaccuracies and omissions at certain points, but its descriptive part is a trustworthy and valuable store of facts. We should assume that the lost *LP* was of similar quality.

The main problem that confronts us here is which sources Plutarch used. Several Spartans are among the subjects of his *Parallel Lives*: Lykourgos, Lysander, Agesilaos, Agis and Kleomenes. Of these Lykourgos was the one who presented far the greatest difficulty to him, because, as he says himself (*Lyk.* 1.1), virtually no undisputed facts were known about the man. Plutarch's object in the *Lives* was not exactly to write history, but to present the characters of famous men and thus to give moral instruction to his readers. But how could he present the character of Lykourgos when so little was known of it? His solution was to recount Lykourgos's legislation, on the assumption that the kind of laws he made showed the kind of man he was. The result is that this book contains the fullest surviving description of Spartan law. But can we trust this account, written at the beginning of the second century A.D., half a millennium after the classical period? Does it give a true picture of 'the laws of Lykourgos' as they really were in the fifth century and earlier, or only of the legend passed on and refined by moralizers over several hundred years? Where did Plutarch get it from?

τῷ μὲν ἀντιδικῶν διατελεῖ, τῷ δὲ συναγορεύων. 'A similar account of these events is given by Phylarkhos, in whom not much trust should be placed if it were not for the testimony of Polybios; for partiality makes him excited whenever he touches on Kleomenes, and, as if at a trial, he constantly argues against the one and in favour of the other in his history.'

In the face of this passage it ought never to have been supposed that Plutarch follows Phylarkhos uncritically, even in those passages where he does make substantial use of him. We should accept that he did have the work of Phylarkhos at hand while he was writing *Agis and Kleomenes*, and selected from it information which was helpful to the ethical purposes of his own book (cf. Gabba *Athenaeum* 35 (1957) 222-4). But even in this book he could adduce Aristotle as his authority when he mentioned a legal point (*Kleom.* 9.3, adducing Arist. fr. 539), and probably made quite extensive use of Aristotle (cf. Marasco *Athenaeum* 56 (1978) 170-81). However, most of the information which Plutarch gives us about Spartan law is not in *Agis and Kleomenes* but in *Lykourgos*; and there is no special reason to think that in writing *Lykourgos* he made use of Phylarkhos, whom in fact he does not mention there. We should therefore reject the view that his references to Spartan law rest on a third-century fabrication. His judgement of his sources was good, and we may use, with due caution, the material which he has gleaned from them.

Finally a few words may be added here about the collection of Lakonian apophthegms preserved in Plutarch's *Ethika* 208a-242d. (For a fuller discussion see Ollier *Mirage* 2.21-54.) It consists of the following parts (as edited and numbered in Nachstädt's Teubner edition). First there are 416 apophthegms attributed to various Spartan men; Agesilaos, with

79, has the largest number, and 72 are anonymous. Next come 'institutions', 42 short paragraphs each recording some interesting Spartan law or custom. Lastly there are 40 apophthegms attributed to Spartan women; 30 of these are anonymous. There is some repetition: several sayings occur more than once, ascribed to different speakers. A few of the items are not actually sayings, but interesting acts by Spartans.

No doubt many of these sayings are more or less fictional. They are laconic remarks put into Lakonic mouths. Yet some originated at least as early as the fourth century: two of those attributed to Agesilaos (nos. 5 and 19, in 208d and 210a) occur also in Xenophon's *Agesilaos* (11.4, 5.2), and one of the anonymous ones (no. 19, in 233b) is found with nearly the same wording in Plato (*Phdr.* 260e). Many of them recur in Plutarch's *Lives*; in particular, his *Lykourgos* has not only many of the apophthegms attributed to Lykourgos but also many of the 'institutions', some of them in a similar sequence (see Nachstädt's table, p. 166). Probably Plutarch compiled the collection in the course of his reading, and later selected items from it to illustrate the characters of the various Spartans in his *Lives*. The best of the sayings are worth reading for their epigrammatic quality rather than for any historical value, but in a few cases they mention or imply something which can be used as evidence of Spartan law.

II

Status

THE THREE CLASSES

The population of Lakonia included three main social classes, whose legal status was distinct: Spartiates, perioikoi, and helots. There were also some minor classes or subdivisions, which will be considered later in this chapter. The origin of the tripartite division is a subject of ancient legend and modern dispute; in particular, it remains uncertain whether the three classes differed racially, as Dorians and non-Dorians. That problem will not be investigated here, where my object is only to define the distinctions of status as they existed in the fifth and fourth centuries. But I begin with Ephoros's account of the origin, as preserved by Strabo, because, although what he says about the remote past is legend rather than history, it is a legend which he thought adequate to explain the state of affairs which existed in his own time, and is thus a reliable indicator of the facts of the fourth century.

Str. 8.5.4 (*F. Gr. Hist.* 70 F117). φησὶ δ' Ἔφορος ... · ὑπακούοντας δ' ἅπαντας τοὺς περιοίκους Σπαρτιατῶν ὅμως ἰσονόμους εἶναι, μετέχοντας καὶ πολιτείας καὶ ἀρχείων· [καλεῖσθαι δὲ εἴλωτας·] Ἆγιν δὲ τὸν Εὐρυσθένους ἀφελέσθαι τὴν ἰσοτιμίαν καὶ συντελεῖν προστάξαι τῇ Σπάρτῃ· τοὺς μὲν οὖν ἄλλους ὑπακοῦσαι, τοὺς δ' Ἑλείους, τοὺς ἔχοντας τὸ Ἕλος, ποιησαμένους ἀπόστασιν κατὰ κράτος ἁλῶναι πολέμῳ καὶ κριθῆναι δούλους ἐπὶ τακτοῖς τισιν, ὥστε τὸν ἔχοντα μήτ' ἐλευθεροῦν ἐξεῖναι μήτε πωλεῖν ἔξω τῶν ὅρων τούτους· τοῦτον δὲ λεχθῆναι τὸν πρὸς τοὺς εἵλωτας πόλεμον. σχεδὸν δέ τι καὶ τὴν εἱλωτείαν τὴν ὕστερον συμμείνασαν μέχρι τῆς Ῥωμαίων ἐπικρατείας οἱ περὶ Ἀγίν εἰσιν οἱ καταδείξαντες· τρόπον γάρ τινα δημοσίους δούλους εἶχον οἱ Λακεδαιμόνιοι τούτους, κατοικίας τινὰς αὐτοῖς ἀποδείξαντες καὶ λειτουργίας ἰδίας. 'Ephoros says . . .; and that all the perioikoi obeyed the Spartiates but were nevertheless equal to them in law, sharing both citizenship and magistracies; [and that they were called helots;] but that Agis, son of Eurysthenes, took away their equality of status and ordered them to be tributaries of Sparta; and that, whereas the rest obeyed, the Heleians, the inhabitants of Helos, revolted, and were forcibly subdued by a war and condemned to slavery on certain conditions, namely that it was not permitted for the holder either to liberate them or to sell them outside the boundaries; and that this was called the war against the helots. In effect, it was Agis and his associates who instituted the helotry which lasted down to the time of the Roman supremacy; for the Lakedaimonians possessed these as a kind of public slaves, fixing for them certain places of residence and particular duties.'

A few comments may be made on details of this text. The infinitives show how far the reporting from Ephoros extends; the last sentence (from σχεδὸν δέ) is Strabo's own addition. The words καλεῖσθαι δὲ εἵλωτας are clearly out of place, because the helots are not introduced until a line or two later; some editors transfer those three words to a later point, but it is better just to delete them, as being some reader's marginal note wrongly copied into the text. The difference in sense between συντελεῖν here and συντελοῦσαν in Plu. *Lyk.* 8.5 (quoted on page 90) is worth noting, because at first sight the two passages seem inconsistent; in Ephoros the verb is used of the perioikoi, meaning that they paid tribute or tax, but in Plutarch it is used of Spartan land and excludes the land of the perioikoi, because it has the sense of administrative connection.

It is clear that Ephoros regarded both the perioikoi and the helots as being subject to the authority of the Spartiates, with the difference that the helots were slaves (δοῦλοι) while the perioikoi were not. Yet even the helots were not slaves in the usual sense, but slaves 'on certain conditions', 'a kind of public slaves'. We need to consider what this meant in terms of particular rights and duties.

It can be taken for granted that the classes were hereditary: a person belonged to the same class as his parents. Persons of mixed parentage, and possibilities of transfer from one class to another, will be mentioned later in this chapter.

SPARTIATES

Only those in the top class were considered citizens of Sparta, and only they are called Σπαρτιᾶται. The term Λακεδαιμόνιοι is ambiguous; sometimes it means the citizens only, sometimes it includes the other classes. The usual phrase for the state or the authorities collectively is οἱ Λακεδαιμόνιοι. (The terminology is examined by Toynbee *Problems* 159-60, Westlake *CQ* 27 (1977) 97-100.) In English it is usual and convenient to use the word 'Spartiate' for a member of the top class. Another term used for it is ὅμοιοι, meaning 'equals' or 'peers' (Xen. *LP* 10.7, 13.1, etc.), a usage which emphasizes that there were no further distinctions within this body. We should therefore reject the suggestion that the phrase οἱ καλοὶ κἀγαθοί in two passages (Arist. *Pol.* 1270b 24, Plu. *Lyk.* 17.2) refers to a legally privileged section within the class of Spartiates (cf. Michell *Sparta* 43).

It seems that, though they could own land elsewhere, the Spartiates all resided in the city. For the city, there is no distinction in meaning between the names Σπάρτη and Λακεδαίμων. It was made up of five villages, which in the time of Thucydides (1.10.2) had still not been physically unified, namely Limnai, Konooura, Mesoa, Pitane, and Amyklai; the last was about twenty stades south of the others (Polyb. 5.19.2-3). (The form Κονοου- is given in inscriptions, *IG* 5(1) 480, 566. Κυνοσουρεῖς in Paus. 3.16.9 should be emended.)

The citizens were organized in divisions for which two names are used, φυλή and ὠβά, usually anglicized as 'tribe' and 'obe' (cf. Plu. *Lyk.* 6.2, quoted on page 3). Inscriptions of the Roman period show that at that time each of the five old villages provided one such division, which could be called either 'tribe' or 'obe' indifferently, so that we find both τῆς Λιμναέων φυλῆς and ὠβὰ Λιμναιέων (*IG* 5(1) 564, 688). There was also by then an obe called Νεοπολῖται (*IG* 5(1) 680, etc.), but since that means 'new citizens' it probably did not exist in the earlier period. Modern scholars have wondered whether further obes existed, but there is no clear evidence of any others (for some doubtful evidence see Beattie *CQ* 45 (1951) 46-58, Forrest *Sparta* 42-3), and it is likelier that there were only the five obes in the fifth and fourth centuries (cf. Wade-Gery *Essays* 69-85, Kiechle *Lakonien* 119-27, Cartledge *Sparta* 107). As for the tribes, their number and nature at that period is uncertain. A fragment of Tyrtaios (19.8 West) refers to Πάμφυλοί τε καὶ Ὑλλεῖς ἠδ[ὲ Δυμᾶνες], which are known to have been names of tribes in other Dorian cities (Hdt. 5.68.2, Steph. Byz. under Δυμᾶνες), and thus may have been tribes in

STATUS

Sparta too. One view (asserted by Wade-Gery *Essays* 70-1, rejected by Forrest *Sparta* 43-4) is that in the archaic period the Spartiates were classified both by heredity, in three tribes, and by place of residence, in five obes. But even if that is right, at some time before the Roman period the three old tribes ceased to exist and the word φυλή came to be applied to the obes instead; no evidence shows when that happened. Bare references to φυλαί or φυλέται (Plu. *Lyk.* 6.2, 16.1) could mean either the old tribes or the later ones; and a reference to phratries in Sparta, quoted from Demetrios of Skepsis by Athenaios (141f, adduced by Wade-Gery *Essays* 79), does not prove the continued existence of the old tribes. The nature of those phratries is likewise obscure.

PERIOIKOI

The perioikoi were the inhabitants of all the cities in Lakonia other than Sparta, together with a few in Messenia and the offshore islands. (For a list of sites see Cartledge *Sparta* 185-93.) Their settlements, though some of them were very small, may be called 'cities' because Greek writers call them πόλεις (e.g. Hdt. 7.234.2, Thuc. 5.54.1, Xen. *LP* 15.3). The significance of this word is that they were formally self-governing and made their own laws. Their laws were not Spartan laws and thus, even if we knew anything about them, would not be part of the subject of this book. Yet the perioikoi do need further attention here, because Ephoros clearly regarded them as subject to the Spartiates and to Spartan law. Isokrates in his Panathenaic speech goes further. He regards the Spartiates as the aristocratic rulers and the perioikoi as the people (δῆμος or πλῆθος) whom the aristocrats have enslaved (12.177-81).

There seem in fact to have been three ways in which Spartan law prevailed over the perioikoi. One was a requirement to perform military service. There is plenty of evidence that Lakedaimonian forces regularly included some perioikoi (e.g. Hdt. 9.11.3, Thuc. 5.54.1, Xen. *Hell.* 6.5.21), and Isokrates alleges that perioikoi not only fought alongside Spartiates but were even sent out by themselves on dangerous missions (12.180). This must mean that when the Spartan authorities called on perioikoi to serve on a campaign they had to do so. One occasion is known when a perioikos was the commander of a number of ships (Thuc. 8.22.1), but that does not prove that a perioikos ever had authority to give orders to Spartiates, since the ships were probably manned by non-Spartiates.

Secondly, landholding. Plutarch says that Lykourgos 'allotted the rest of Lakonia to the perioikoi in 30,000 lots' (*Lyk.* 8.5, quoted on page 90). This does not necessarily mean that those lots were all equal, still less that Lykourgos measured them and drew the boundaries. It can be taken as meaning simply that the Spartiates permitted the perioikoi to occupy the whole of Lakonia except the land pertaining to the city of Sparta, and that that area contained 30,000 farms or landholdings, the figure being no doubt just an estimate. Estates in the districts of a number of the cities of perioikoi were held by the Spartan kings (Xen. *LP* 15.3). The only other way in which Spartan law was concerned with land belonging to the perioikoi is that the perioikoi were required to pay tribute or tax (συντελεῖν in Ephoros, quoted on page 23). Land was the basis of taxation in Sparta (Arist. *Pol.* 1271b 13-15); so the tribute paid by the perioikoi was probably a tax on landholdings, though there is no evidence to show how it was calculated or in what form it was paid.

Thirdly, jurisdiction. Isokrates declares that the cities of perioikoi in Lakonia have less power than the demes in Attika (12.179); but that should be interpreted as meaning that they were not represented in the government of Sparta, and not as evidence that they could not manage their own internal affairs. Evidence that the Spartans appointed harmosts or governors (ἁρμοσταί) for them is presented by Parke *Hermathena* 46 (1931) 31-8 and Bockisch *Klio* 46 (1965) 131-7, but it does not amount to much. There is a scholiast's note saying ἦσαν δὲ ἁρμοσταὶ Λακεδαιμονίων εἴκοσιν (schol. on Pind. *Ol.* 6.154), which could mean 'There were twenty harmosts of the Lakedaimonians'; but it could equally well mean 'There were twenty Lakedaimonian harmosts', and thus could be a reference to the governors sent to various places abroad at the end of the Peloponnesian War (Xen. *Hell.* 1.2.18, 3.1.4, etc.). In other texts the term is not used in connection with cities in Lakonia, and some individuals whom Bockisch identifies as harmosts are more correctly to be regarded as commanders of military garrisons, not as governors having jurisdiction over the local population. Thus Brasidas at Methone was φρουρὰν ἔχων (Thuc. 2.25.2); Tantalos at Thyrea was probably sent to the town merely to organize its defence on the occasion of an Athenian attack (Thuc. 4.57.3; he is called a φρούραρχος in Diod. 12.65.9); a reference to τοῖς ἐπ' Αὐλῶνος probably means the military commanders of a Spartan garrison stationed at Aulon (Xen. *Hell.* 3.3.10; cf. Cartledge *Sparta* 274-5); and Geranor at Asine was not a harmost but a πολέμαρχος (Xen. *Hell.* 7.1.25). So it remains doubtful whether it was normal for the cities of the perioikoi to have a Spartiate governor. However, there is good evidence that there was a Spartiate judicial officer for the island of Kythera.

> Thuc. 4.53.2. τὰ δὲ Κύθηρα νῆσός ἐστιν, ἐπίκειται δὲ τῇ Λακωνικῇ κατὰ Μαλέαν· Λακεδαιμόνιοι δ' εἰσὶ τῶν περιοίκων, καὶ κυθηροδίκης ἀρχὴ ἐκ τῆς Σπάρτης διέ-

βαινεν αὐτόσε κατὰ ἔτος. 'Kythera is an island, and it lies off Lakonia opposite Malea. The inhabitants are Lakedaimonians, belonging to the perioikoi, and a magistrate called *kytherodikes* used to go across there from Sparta every year.'

The phrase ἐκ τῆς Σπάρτης means that the magistrate was a Spartiate, and the name κυθηροδίκης implies that his primary function was to judge cases for the people of Kythera. He is not to be regarded as a military commander. κατὰ ἔτος may mean either that the office was held by a different man each year, or that one assize was held each year, or more probably both. The special title of the magistrate, and the fact that Thucydides considers him worth mentioning, indicates that this was a unique arrangement for Kythera, not shared by other cities of the perioikoi; no place but Kythera can have had a κυθηροδίκης. But there is nothing to show why it was thought desirable that Kythera alone should have a visiting Spartiate judge. The past tense διέβαινεν implies that the arrangement had been discontinued when Thucydides wrote about it; it must have ceased when the Athenians occupied the island in 424, but the possibility remains open that it was resumed after the Spartans regained possession. (A fourth-century inscription from Kythera records a dedication by 'Menandros, harmost' (*IG* 5(1) 937), but it does not say what place Menandros governed, and Cartledge *Sparta* 244 is too hasty in identifying him with the fifth-century κυθηροδίκης.)

The ephors also had powers of jurisdiction over perioikoi.

Isok. 12.181. ἔξεστι τοῖς ἐφόροις ἀκρίτους ἀποκτεῖναι τοσούτους ὁπόσους ἂν βουληθῶσιν. 'The ephors are permitted to put to death without trial as many (perioikoi) as they wish.'

We know of one occasion when the ephors gave orders for the arrest of some perioikoi at Aulon, though in that particular case the orders were a ruse for sending Kinadon out of Sparta and the ephors did not expect them to be carried out (Xen. *Hell.* 3.3.8). It is unlikely that the ephors or their emissaries regularly toured the cities of perioikoi and carried out executions indiscriminately. But it is quite plausible that, if a perioikos was caught committing an offence in Sparta, the five ephors had authority to judge him and impose whatever penalty they thought fit. If they were authorized to act without reference to a full court of law in formal session, that does not necessarily mean that they acted without due investigation and concern for justice. (Cf. Bonner and Smith *CP* 37 (1942) 122.) Jones *Sparta* 8 considers that Isokrates is wrong about this; 'he is mixing up the Perioeci with the Helots'. But that is not so, for the rule about the helots was different: the point of the annual declaration of war on the helots (see pages 36-7) was that it entitled any Spartiate, not merely the ephors, to kill them. So the statement of Isokrates about the perioikoi should be accepted. But beyond this we remain totally ignorant about the legal rights of perioikoi when they had dealings with Spartiates or were within the territory of the city of Sparta.

HELOTS

The first helots were apparently resident in Lakonia, though the origin of the institution and the name is not now ascertainable (cf. Lotze Μεταξὺ ἐλευθέρων καὶ δούλων 26-7, Ducat *Anc. Soc.* 9 (1978) 5-13). After the Spartans conquered Messenia, most of the people of that country were made helots too, so that in the fifth century the helots of Messenia outnumbered the others (Thuc. 1.101.2). In 369 Messenia became independent again, but in Lakonia there continued to be helots. They were not exactly slaves, and it is difficult to give a precise definition of their status; it is not satisfactory to assume that they were the same as medieval serfs or villeins (cf. Oliva *Sparta* 38-48, Ducat *Anc. Soc.* 9 (1978) 13-24). It is better to proceed by seeing what they did and what they could not do.

Their chief function was agriculture: they farmed the land held by the Spartiates and gave them part of the produce, keeping the rest for themselves.

> Myron (*F. Gr. Hist.* 106) F2 (from Ath. 657d). καὶ παραδόντες αὐτοῖς τὴν χώραν ἔταξαν μοῖραν ἣν αὐτοῖς ἀνοίσουσιν ἀεί. 'They (the Spartiates) handed over their land to them (the helots) and fixed the portion which they should always render to them.'

> Plu. *Lyk.* 24.2 οἱ δ' εἵλωτες αὐτοῖς εἰργάζοντο τὴν γῆν, ἀποφορὰν τὴν εἰρημένην τελοῦντες. 'The helots worked the land for them, paying over a stated amount of the proceeds.'

> Plu. *Eth.* 239d-e. οἱ δὲ εἵλωτες αὐτοῖς εἰργάζοντο τὴν γῆν ἀποφορὰν τὴν ἄνωθεν ἱσταμένην ⟨τελοῦντες⟩. ἐπάρατον δ' ἦν πλείονός τινα μισθῶσαι, ἵν' ἐκεῖνοι μὲν κερδαίνοντες ἡδέως ὑπηρετῶσιν, αὐτοὶ δὲ μὴ πλέον ἐπιζητῶσιν. 'The helots worked the land for them, paying over an amount of the proceeds which was settled from the start. A curse was laid on anyone who charged more, in order that they (the helots) might serve gladly because they were making a profit, and (the citizens) themselves might not try to get more.'

There is doubt whether the payment made by the helots to the Spartiate landholder was a fixed amount or a fixed proportion of the crops. The latter part of the passage quoted from Plu. *Eth.* 239d-e implies that the helots kept all the surplus above a fixed amount; that was their incentive to maximize the produce. If that is right, it is reasonable to presume from the figures given in Plu. *Lyk.* 8.7 (quoted on pages 90-1) that the amount was 82 medimnoi of barley annually, plus a fixed amount of liquid products (wine, milk, olive oil), from each lot in Lakonia; different amounts must have been fixed for lots of different sizes in Messenia. But the required payment is stated in Paus. 4.14.4 and Ael. *Var. Hist.* 6.1 to have been a half of the crops. Pausanias and Aelian both go straight on to mention that helots had to attend the funerals of prominent Spartiates, and it is clear that they are both drawing on a poem of Tyrtaios which mentions these two subjects consecutively, and which Pausanias quotes. Thus this poem is the true source of the information.

> Tyrtaios fr. 6-7 (West) (from Paus. 4.14.5).
> ὥσπερ ὄνοι μεγάλοις ἄχθεσι τειρόμενοι,
> δεσποσύνοισι φέροντες ἀναγκαίης ὕπο λυγρῆς
> ἥμισυ †πάνθ' ὅσσων καρπὸν ἄρουρα φέρει,
> δεσπότας οἰμώζοντες, ὁμῶς ἄλοχοί τε καὶ αὐτοί,
> εὖτέ τιν' οὐλομένη μοῖρα κίχοι θανάτου.
>
> 'Like donkeys, oppressed with great burdens; bringing to their masters, under grim compulsion, half . . . of what the soil bears as fruit; their wives and themselves alike lamenting their masters, whenever the dire fate of death befalls any of them.'

πάνθ' is ungrammatical and must be wrong. Various emendations have been suggested, including ἥμισυ πᾶν, 'an entire half . . .' (Wilamowitz); but nearer than this to the manuscripts' text is ἥμισυ πᾶν θ', 'half and the whole' (Allen, adopted in Rocha-Pereira's Teubner edition of Pausanias), meaning that some helots handed over half and some the whole of their produce. These readings, especially the latter, look like poetic rhetoric, and make it doubtful whether the passage can be used as evidence that a half was a legal figure; rather, Tyrtaios is exclaiming that the required payment worked out in practice at half of the crop in many instances. So it is preferable to keep to the view that the helots had to pay over a fixed amount of their produce, rather than a fixed proportion, at least from the equal lots of land in Lakonia; in Messenia, where farms may have varied in size, the system may have been different.

It should be noticed that a Spartiate who demanded more than his permitted share was subject to a curse rather than to any penalty imposed by the state (Plu. *Eth.* 239d-e). In practice helots' rights could not be enforced against Spartiates. Nevertheless the existence of the law, even if not adequately enforced, does imply a recognition that helots had some rights, including a right to own goods. Their capacity to own is confirmed by the fact that Kleomenes III in 223 offered freedom to any helot who paid 5 mnai, and in this way collected 500 talents, which means that 6000 helots were able to produce that quite large fee (Plu. *Kleom.* 23.1; the figure has been doubted, but cf. Africa *CSCA* 1 (1968) 4).

Capacity to own goods, then, is one way in which the legal position of helots differed from that of slaves in Athens and elsewhere. In Athens slaves were themselves legally goods owned by someone else, and anything which a slave had was legally the property of the slave's owner and could not be kept or spent by the slave without his owner's consent; in Sparta helots were not in so ignominious a situation. There were also other ways in which the legal authority of a Spartiate over the helots on his land was less than that of an owner of slaves. According to Ephoros (quoted on page 24) he was not permitted 'either to liberate them or to sell them outside the boundaries'.

The rule about liberation is clear. An individual Spartiate could not declare a helot free. The state, however, could and sometimes did, usually to reward helots who fought well for Sparta in war (Thuc. 4.80.3, 5.34.1, Xen. *Hell.* 6.5.28). In this sense helots belonged to the state, not to an individual (δοῦλοι τοῦ κοινοῦ in Paus. 3.20.6; cf. Strabo's δημοσίους δούλους in his comment on the passage of Ephoros). Less clear is the rule about sale. Did the ban on selling helots 'outside the boundaries' (ἔξω τῶν ὅρων) mean that a Spartiate could sell a helot to another Spartiate within Lakonia or Messenia? That interpretation is not explicitly contradicted by other evidence; and yet it does not fit well with the impression we otherwise have that helots were able to stay put and run their own farms as long as they delivered the required amount of produce, and that the individual Spartiate was not entitled to make further personal profits out of them. I am therefore inclined to interpret ἔξω τῶν ὅρων as a reference not to the national frontiers but to the boundaries of an individual lot of land (κλῆρος). The phrase explains πωλεῖν rather than modifies it: the Spartiate could not sell a helot and thus remove him from his land.

This also fits better with Strabo's comment that the Lakedaimonians fixed for the helots 'certain places of residence and particular duties'. His phrase οἱ Λακεδαιμόνιοι should be taken as meaning the state, not the individual Spartiates; the state decided where the helots were to live and work, and the individual Spartiate had no legal power to change those arrangements. It is consistent with this that helots were also required to perform military or naval service for Sparta from time to time (e.g. Hdt. 9.10.1, Thuc. 7.19.3, Xen. *Hell.* 7.1.12; cf. Welwei *Unfreie* 1.108-81). But when they were at home, the law required each Spartiate landholder to keep the helots on his land in proper order and control.

Myron (*F. Gr. Hist.* 106) F2 (from Ath. 657d). τοῖς δ' εἵλωσι πᾶν ὑβριστικὸν ἔργον ἐπιτάττουσι πρὸς πᾶσαν ἄγον ἀτιμίαν. κυνῆν τε γὰρ ἕκαστον φορεῖν ἐπάναγκες ὥρισαν καὶ διφθέραν περιβεβλῆσθαι πληγάς τε τεταγμένας λαμβάνειν κατ' ἐνιαυτὸν ἀδικήματος χωρίς, ἵνα μήποτε δουλεύειν ἀπομάθωσιν. πρὸς δὲ τούτοις εἴ τινες ὑπερακμάζοιεν τὴν οἰκετικὴν ἐπιφάνειαν, ἐπέθηκαν ζημίαν θάνατον καὶ τοῖς κεκτημένοις ἐπιτίμιον, εἰ μὴ ἐπικόπτοιεν τοὺς ἁδρουμένους. 'On the helots they imposed any insulting task which was conducive to any indignity. They laid it down as compulsory that each should wear a dogskin cap and a leather jerkin, and should be beaten a fixed number of strokes annually, apart from any offence, so that they might never forget they were slaves. In addition, if any overstepped the appearance suitable for a slave, they imposed the death penalty, with a fine for the masters if they did not check those who were becoming sturdy.'

Thus there were laws about the clothes which helots should wear, and about annual beatings. The law prescribing a penalty for a Spartiate who failed to keep his helots down is rather like modern laws about dangerous animals, under which an animal which gets out of control is killed and its owner fined. Helots likewise could be a danger to the Spartan community. But they were not in fact regarded as animals, but as human beings. Consequently they were the subject of an annual declaration of war.

Plu. *Lyk.* 28.7 (Arist. fr. 538). Ἀριστοτέλης δὲ μάλιστά φησι καὶ τοὺς ἐφόρους, ὅταν εἰς τὴν ἀρχὴν καταστῶσι πρῶτον, τοῖς εἵλωσι καταγγέλλειν πόλεμον, ὅπως εὐαγὲς ᾖ τὸ ἀνελεῖν. 'Aristotle in particular says also that the ephors, as soon as they enter office, declare war on the helots, so that killing them may not be impious.'

A declaration of war by the ephors was one made on behalf of the state as a whole. It entitled anyone to kill those who were declared enemies, and it must have had both religious and legal significance: the killer of an enemy would not be polluted in a religious sense and also would not be liable to legal proceedings for homicide. Thus no guilt was attached to any Spartiate who killed a helot; and the Spartan 'secret service' (κρυπτεία), described in Plu. *Lyk*. 28, regularly put helots to death, especially those who were exceptionally strong. Isokrates declares 'The Lakedaimonians have put more Greeks to death without trial than have been put on trial in Athens since the foundation of our city' (12.66); he cannot have had any statistics, but his statement may well be true. (When Bonner and Smith *CP* 37 (1942) 122 say 'This cannot be true', they are thinking only of the perioikoi and have forgotten the helots.) The same declaration of war gave an individual Spartan virtually unlimited powers to punish his helots, because he could put to death with a clear conscience any helot who did not submit to any other punishment which he imposed. As between a Spartiate and a helot, the law was always on the Spartiate's side.

SLAVES

It has been doubted whether the Spartans had any slaves other than helots. General references to δοῦλοι and δοῦλαι (as in Xen. *LP* 1.4) can be interpreted as meaning helots. But there is some evidence that there were other slaves too. One passage mentions the Spartans' superiority over Athens 'in ownership of slaves, both others and helots' (Pl. *Alk.* 122d). Another says that they left their money-making 'to slaves and helots' (Plu. *Comp. Lyk. Num.* 2.7). Thucydides, recounting the conclusion of the revolt at Ithome in the middle of the fifth century, says that the rebels, who consisted of helots and some perioikoi (1.101.2), surrendered on condition that they should leave the Peloponnese and never return; ἢν δέ τις ἁλίσκηται, τοῦ λαβόντος εἶναι δοῦλον, 'if anyone was caught, he was to be the slave of his captor' (1.103.1). One would expect the penalty for a helot caught in the Peloponnese to be something worse than merely becoming a helot again. Elsewhere Thucydides calls the helots εἵλωτες, and it is unlikely that he would have used the word δοῦλος here unless he meant something different. There is also the evidence of five inscriptions from the temple of Poseidon at Tainaron, dating from the second half of the fifth century or the first half of the fourth (*IG* 5(1) 1228-32). I quote only the first; the others have fairly similar wording.

> *IG* 5(1) 1228. ἀνέθεκε τοῖ Παhοιδᾶ[νι] Θεάρες Κλεογένε. ἔφορος Δαίοχος. ἐπάκο Ἀρίο(ν), Λύον.
> 'Theares dedicated Kleogenes to Poseidon. Ephor: Daiokhos. Witnesses: Arion, Lyon.'

This is most easily interpreted as meaning that Theares liberated his slave Kleogenes in the year in which Daiokhos was the chief ephor at Sparta. It cannot be the liberation of a helot, because helots could be liberated only by the state, not by an individual. Theares could be either a Spartiate or a perioikos, but Cartledge *Sparta* 179, seems to have no good reason for saying that these inscriptions 'must be attributed to Perioikoi', and the naming of the Spartan ephor makes it more likely that Theares was a Spartiate.

We should therefore accept (despite the objections of Lotze Μεταξὺ ἐλευθέρων καὶ δούλων 35-40; cf. Oliva *Sparta* 172-4, Welwei *Unfreie* 1.108-9) that Spartiates did have personal slaves in addition to helots, though not necessarily in large numbers. They may have been captured in war, bought from traders, or descendants of slaves acquired in those ways. They will have been used mainly for household services. (The Spartiates' houses were in the city, whereas the helots mostly lived in the countryside.) There is no further information about the legal position of these slaves, but presumably it was like that of slaves elsewhere: they were legally the property of their owners, who could sell them, or liberate them, or do whatever else they wished with them.

FREEDMEN

A remarkably long list of special Spartan terms for liberated slaves is given in another fragment of the lost historian Myron of Priene.

> Myron (*F. Gr. Hist.* 106) F1 (from Ath. 271f). πολλάκις ἠλευθέρωσαν Λακεδαιμόνιοι δούλους, καὶ οὓς μὲν ἀφέτας ἐκάλεσαν, οὓς δὲ ἀδεσπότους, οὓς δὲ ἐρυκτῆρας, δεσποσιοναύτας δ' ἄλλους οὓς εἰς τοὺς στόλους κατέτασσον, ἄλλους δὲ νεοδαμώδεις ἑτέρους ὄντας τῶν εἱλώτων. 'The Lakedaimonians often liberated slaves, and they called some *aphetai*, and some *adespotoi*, and some *erykteres*, and others whom they posted on naval operations *desposionautai*, and others *neodamodeis*, who were distinct from the helots [or: and other different ones *neodamodeis*, who were some of the helots].'

The first four of these terms are otherwise unknown. Some of them may have been colloquial rather than technical; it is not necessary to try to think up legal distinctions between them. The neodamodeis, on the other hand, were of considerable importance, at least in the late fifth and early fourth centuries, when they formed a significant part of the Spartan army (Thuc. 7.19.3, 8.5.1, Xen. *Hell.* 3.1.4, etc.). How was this class legally defined? Definitions are given in two lexicons.

> Polydeukes 3.83. τοὺς μέντοι εἰς ἐλευθερίαν τῶν εἰλώτων ἀφιεμένους οἱ Λακεδαιμόνιοι νεοδαμώδεις καλοῦσιν. 'Those of the helots who are released into freedom are called by the Lakedaimonians *neodamodeis*.'

> Hesykhios ν 314. νεοδαμώδεις· οἱ κατὰ δόσιν ἐλεύθεροι ἀπὸ τῆς εἰλωτίας. '*Neodamodeis*: those given freedom from helotry.'

These definitions say clearly that a neodamodes was a liberated helot, and so it is best to interpret Myron in accordance with this; the difficult last words of the fragment of Myron may be taken as meaning that a neodamodes was a liberated helot, whereas the other four words which he lists mean liberated slaves (not necessarily excluding liberated helots).

But there are two difficulties about this definition. The first is the etymology of the word, which must be derived from νέος and δᾶμος. If a neodamodes was a new member of the people, does that mean that a liberated helot became a full Spartan citizen (the view of Kahrstedt *Staatsrecht* 1.46)? No, it cannot mean that, because the passages where Thucydides and Xenophon mention neodamodeis (especially Xen. *Hell.* 3.3.6) make clear that their status was inferior to the status of Spartiates. We must accept that this is one of the many words of which the etymology is not a reliable guide to political or legal facts. The second difficulty arises from the earliest reference to neodamodeis.

Thuc. 5.34.1. οἱ Λακεδαιμόνιοι ἐψηφίσαντο τοὺς μὲν μετὰ Βρασίδου εἴλωτας μαχεσαμένους ἐλευθέρους εἶναι καὶ οἰκεῖν ὅπου ἂν βούλωνται, καὶ ὕστερον οὐ πολλῷ αὐτοὺς μετὰ τῶν νεοδαμώδων ἐς Λέπρεον κατέστησαν. 'The Lakedaimonians voted that the helots who had fought under Brasidas should be free and should reside wherever they wished; and not long afterwards they settled them, together with the neodamodeis, at Lepreon.'

In this passage (and again in 5.67.1) Thucydides clearly distinguishes between the neodamodeis and the helots liberated for their service under Brasidas. So not all liberated helots were neodamodeis. But what distinguished them? One suggestion, made by Willetts *CP* 49 (1954) 27-32, is that the neodamodeis were helots living on estates which had been left without a Spartiate heir; they were allowed, Willetts suggests, to retain the land for themselves on condition that they performed hoplite service. But this is refuted by the passage of Thucydides; if the neodamodeis had had land in Lakonia, they would not have wanted to be given land in the recently annexed area of Lepreon. (I do not accept the view of Welwei *Unfreie* 1.145, that the settlement at Lepreon countermanded the permission to reside wherever they wished; καί is not adversative.) Another suggestion, made by Tonini *RIL* 109 (1975) 305-16, is that they were hoplites settled in frontier territory as a garrison; but that fails to explain the distinction made by Thucydides between the neodamodeis and the Brasidean ex-helots, since both those groups were settled at Lepreon. Perhaps, rather, the thing which distinguished the neodamodeis from other liberated helots was military training; a suggestion on these lines will be made later in this chapter (page 51).

We can assume that all liberated helots and slaves could continue to reside in Spartan territory, but could not take part in politics. Their position may have been much like that of metics in Athens, but in one respect perhaps they were better off: Thuc. 5.34.1, about the settlement at Lepreon, implies that they were permitted to own land, whereas in Athens the right to own land (ἔγκτησις γῆς), though sometimes given to individuals as a privilege, was not possessed by metics in general.

DISFRANCHISED SPARTIATES

It was a fundamental principle of 'the laws of Lykourgos' that a man lost his status as a citizen if he failed to keep to the Spartiates' way of life. In particular, during his boyhood he had to go through the training called the *agoge*; as an adult, he had to be a member of a mess, paying his contributions to it and taking his meals in it; and he had to show proper courage in war. This way of life is sometimes called τὰ καλά (Xen. *LP* 3.3, *Hell.* 5.3.9, Plu. *Agis* 5.5), which I translate 'the life of honour'. It included both toils and privileges, and a man who deviated from it ceased to be a Spartiate peer. (Toynbee *Problems* 161 thinks that a man who ceased to be ὅμοιος would still have been Σπαρτιάτης, but to maintain this he has to say that Xenophon has made a mistake in *Hell.* 3.3.5-6, where the terms are treated as synonyms.) The principle is mentioned twice by Xenophon.

> Xen. *LP* 3.3. ἐπιθεὶς δὲ καὶ εἴ τις ταῦτα φύγοι, μηδενὸς ἔτι τῶν καλῶν τυγχάνειν, ἐποίησε μὴ μόνον τοὺς ἐκ δημοσίου ἀλλὰ καὶ τοὺς κηδομένους ἑκάστων ἐπιμελεῖσθαι, ὡς μὴ ἀποδειλιάσαντες ἀδόκιμοι παντάπασιν ἐν τῇ πόλει γένοιντο. 'Laying down that any (of the youths) who evaded these toils should be entirely

excluded from the life of honour, he (Lykourgos) arranged for them to be supervised not only by the men publicly appointed but also by those personally connected with each of them, so that they might not, by flinching, lose all their standing in the city.'

Xen. *LP* 10.7. ἐπέθηκε δὲ καὶ τὴν ἀνυπόστατον ἀνάγκην ἀσκεῖν ἅπασαν πολιτικὴν ἀρετήν. τοῖς μὲν γὰρ τὰ νόμιμα ἐκτελοῦσιν ὁμοίως ἅπασι τὴν πόλιν οἰκείαν ἐποίησε, καὶ οὐδὲν ὑπελογίσατο οὔτε σωμάτων οὔτε χρημάτων ἀσθένειαν· εἰ δέ τις ἀποδειλιάσειε τοῦ τὰ νόμιμα διαπονεῖσθαι, τοῦτον ἐκεῖνος ἀπέδειξε μηδὲ νομίζεσθαι ἔτι τῶν ὁμοίων εἶναι. 'He (Lykourgos) also imposed the irresistible compulsion to practise every virtue of a citizen. He gave equal rights in the city to all who performed the legal requirements, and he took no account of inferiority either in physique or in property; but he laid down that anyone who flinched from the labours required by law was no longer to be considered to be one of the peers.'

Can we define more exactly what Xenophon means by 'the legal requirements'? That they included the *agoge* is clear from 3.3. The *agoge* will be considered in more detail in Chapter III. Only the son and heir of a king was exempt from it (Plu. *Ages.* 1.4). The requirement to belong to a mess is not mentioned by Xenophon, but it is stated in Arist. *Pol.* 1271a 26-37 (quoted on pages 111-12). This topic will be considered in Chapter VI. Spartiates were forbidden by law to engage in menial work or crafts to make money (Xen. *LP* 7.2, Plu. *Lyk.* 24.2, quoted on page 117); no text states the penalty for this, but probably any Spartiate who did it regularly would have been excluded from citizenship because he was not living 'the life of honour'. It is likely that loss of citizenship could also result from condemnation for a serious offence. This is suggested by the case of Kleandridas, who was condemned to death for treason (Plu. *Per.* 22.3-4); his son Gylippos is said by Aelian to have been a mothax (see pages 47-9), which means that the family of Kleandridas had been deprived of Spartiate status.

Cowardice in battle was a cause of ἀτιμία, but the question arises whether that just meant 'dishonour' or involved legal disabilities. Herodotos and Xenophon describe a kind of social ostracism to which a coward was subjected (Hdt. 7.231, Xen. *LP* 9.4-6). But Thucydides, describing action taken against the Spartans who surrendered at Sphakteria, after they returned home, clearly uses ἀτιμία to mean a loss of specific rights.

> Thuc. 5.34.2. ἤδη καὶ ἀρχάς τινας ἔχοντας ἀτίμους ἐποίησαν, ἀτιμίαν δὲ τοιάνδε ὥστε μήτε ἄρχειν μήτε πριαμένους τι ἢ πωλοῦντας κυρίους εἶναι. ὕστερον δὲ αὖθις χρόνῳ ἐπίτιμοι ἐγένοντο. 'Even though they already held some offices, they were disfranchised. The effect of the disfranchisement was that they could not hold office, and had no authority to buy or sell anything. But later on they were enfranchised again.'

Plutarch, recounting the aftermath of the battle of Leuktra in 371, in which many Spartans had been killed, praises Agesilaos for advising the Spartans not to enforce the laws against those who saved their skins, who were called τρέσαντες, 'tremblers': 'the laws must be allowed to sleep today, but must be valid from tomorrow onwards' (*Ages.* 30.2-6). (A similar amnesty was declared after the battle of Megalopolis in 331, according to Diod. 19.70.5.) Plutarch gives details of the penalties which 'tremblers' normally suffered.

Plu. *Ages.* 30.3-4. οὐ γὰρ μόνον ἀρχῆς ἀπείργονται πάσης, ἀλλὰ καὶ δοῦναί τινι τούτων γυναῖκα καὶ λαβεῖν ἄδοξόν ἐστι· παίει δ' ὁ βουλόμενος αὐτοὺς τῶν ἐντυγχανόντων. οἱ δὲ καρτεροῦσι περιιόντες αὐχμηροὶ καὶ ταπεινοί, τρίβωνάς τε προσερραμμένους χρώματος βαπτοῦ φοροῦσι, καὶ ξυρῶνται μέρος τῆς ὑπήνης, μέρος δὲ τρέφουσι. 'Not only are they excluded from every office, but also to give a woman in marriage to any of them, or to accept one, is ignominious; and any passer-by who wishes hits them. They put up with going around in a dirty and abject state; they wear cloaks with coloured patches, and they shave one part of their moustaches and grow the other part.'

From this we may deduce three rules of law. A Spartiate found guilty of cowardice was not allowed to hold office; perhaps he was excluded from all political activities, including attendance at meetings of the assembly, though neither Thucydides nor Plutarch says that. Secondly, any contract of sale which he made was invalid. Since nothing else is known about the law of sale in Sparta, we cannot be sure exactly what that meant; presumably, if he arranged to buy or sell something and the other party to the sale held on to both the money and the goods, he had no legal recourse. Thirdly, he could not retaliate, physically or by legal procedure, if he was struck by anyone; this surely means by any Spartiate (cf. Xen. *LP* 9.5 πληγὰς ὑπὸ τῶν ἀμεινόνων ληπτέον). The rest looks like custom rather than law. Marrying a coward's daughter or giving one's daughter to him in marriage was demeaning (ἄδοξον) but not illegal. The adoption of a ridiculous style of dress and shaving is the kind of thing which the coward's fellows would impose on him informally, by exercising their right to hit him if he did not fall in with it.

Thucydides says that the men from Sphakteria had their rights restored to them later. This may have been a special concession made to those particular men. (There was probably some doubt or disagreement whether they were really cowards; for Thucydides makes clear that the penalty was not imposed on them until they had been back in Sparta for some time and some had been elected to office. Cf. Lewis *Sparta and Persia* 31.) We do not know whether normally disfranchisement for cowardice was permanent or for a limited period, or whether reenfranchisement could be earned by a display of bravery on a later campaign. There is also much else which is obscure about disfranchisement. Did the various kinds of fault (failure to complete the *agoge*, failure to contribute to a mess, condemnation for an offence, cowardice in war) all incur precisely the same penalties, or were different rights lost by men in the different categories? Was disfranchisement always hereditary, or could the son of a coward, for example, be a peer? Xenophon in one passage mentions τοῖς ὑπομείοσι, 'the inferiors' (*Hell.* 3.3.6): does that term cover men in all the categories considered here, or only some of them? Lack of evidence leaves us quite in the dark about these questions.

MOTHAKES

It was possible for a boy who was not of Spartiate birth to be put through the *agoge*. The standard word for such a person was μόθαξ, although this word is not used by Xenophon in the passage which is probably the earliest reference to the practice.

Xen. *Hell.* 5.3.9. πολλοὶ δὲ αὐτῷ καὶ τῶν περιοίκων ἐθελονταὶ καλοὶ κἀγαθοὶ ἠκολούθουν, καὶ ξένοι τῶν τροφίμων καλουμένων, καὶ νόθοι τῶν Σπαρτιατῶν, μάλα εὐειδεῖς τε καὶ τῶν ἐν τῇ πόλει καλῶν οὐκ ἄπειροι. 'He

(Agesipolis) was also accompanied by a large number of volunteers of good quality from the perioikoi, and foreigners from the so-called *trophimoi*, and bastard sons of Spartiates, of very good appearance, and not without experience of the life of honour at Sparta.'

'The life of honour at Sparta' means the life led by Spartiates (see page 42), and the term τρόφιμος, 'fosterling', must mean that the foreigners in question had been reared alongside Spartiate boys. So this passage seems to be referring to an arrangement which is more clearly explained by two later authors.

Phylarkhos (*F. Gr. Hist.* 81) F43 (from Ath. 271e-f). εἰσὶ δ' οἱ μόθακες σύντροφοι τῶν Λακεδαιμόνιων. ἕκαστος γὰρ τῶν πολιτικῶν παίδων, †ὡς ἂν καὶ τὰ ἴδια ἐκποιῶσιν†, οἱ μὲν ἕνα, οἱ δὲ δύο, τινὲς δὲ πλείους ποιοῦνται συντρόφους αὐτῶν. εἰσὶν οὖν οἱ μόθακες ἐλεύθεροι μέν, οὐ μὴν Λακεδαιμόνιοί γε, μετέχουσιν δὲ τῆς παιδείας πάσης. τούτων ἕνα φασὶ γενέσθαι καὶ Λύσανδρον τὸν καταναυμαχήσαντα τοὺς Ἀθηναίους, πολίτην γενόμενον δι' ἀνδραγαθίαν. 'The mothakes are foster-brothers of the Lakedaimonians. The boys of citizen status each ... make some boys their foster-brothers — some one, others two, and some more. The mothakes are free, though not Lakedaimonians, but they share all the education. They say that one of these was Lysander, who defeated the Athenian navy, after he had been made a citizen for his courage.'

Ael. *Var. Hist.* 12.43. Καλλικρατίδας γε μὴν καὶ Γύλιππος καὶ Λύσανδρος ἐν Λακεδαίμονι μόθακες ἐκαλοῦντο. ὄνομα δὲ ἦν ἄρα τοῦτο τοῖς τῶν εὐπόρων ⟨συντρόφοις⟩, οὓς συνεξέπεμπον αὐτοῖς οἱ πατέρες συναγωνιουμένους ἐν τοῖς γυμνασίοις. ὁ δὲ συγχωρήσας τοῦτο Λυκοῦργος τοῖς ἐμμείνασι τῇ τῶν παίδων ἀγωγῇ πολιτείας Λακωνικῆς μεταλαγχάνει. 'Kallikratidas, Gylippos, and Lysander in Lakedaimon were called *mothakes*. This was the name of the foster-brothers of the affluent, whom their fathers sent with them to compete with them in the gymnasiums. The man who made this arrangement, Lykourgos, granted Lakonian citizenship to those who kept to the boys' *agoge*.' (The insertion of συντρόφοις is proposed by Lotze *Historia* 11 (1962) 429.)

It is clear that μόθαξ is the official Spartan term, which Phylarkhos and Aelian consider to require explanation; σύντροφος is not an official term but the ordinary word for a person brought up with another. Only Xenophon offers the term τρόφιμος: either this is an older term, later replaced by μόθαξ, or it has a narrower sense, meaning a mothax of foreign birth. In Plu. *Kleom.* 8.1, a passage referring to two men who were σύντροφοι of Kleomenes III in the third century, Valckenaer's emendation μόθακας (for the manuscripts' σαμοθράκας) is generally accepted; but the reading and interpretation of that passage remain doubtful, because an heir to the kingship would not normally have gone through the *agoge* (Plu. *Ages.* 1.4), and indeed by that period the *agoge* had more or less ceased (Plu. *Agis* 4.2). Later scholia and lexicons give the form μόθων instead of μόθαξ (schol. on Ar. *Knights* 634, *Wealth* 279, Hesykhios μ 1544, *Souda* μ 1188, σ 630); that may be a genuine alternative form, but more probably the Spartan word μόθαξ became confused in later times with the Attic word μόθων meaning 'braggart'. The word κάσεν occurs in inscriptions of the Roman period (*IG* 5(1) 60.4, 71a.7, etc.), but whether that means the same kind of boy as μόθαξ (as maintained by Chrimes *Sparta* 221-3) remains uncertain.

What boys could become mothakes? It is likely that they were of at least three kinds. First, as the passage of Xenophon indicates, there were foreigners. He should have known; he sent his own sons to be brought up in Sparta, on the advice of Agesilaos (Plu. *Ages.* 20.2, Diog. Laert. 2.54). Phokion too sent his son to undergo the *agoge* (Plu. *Phok.* 20.4), and Pyrrhos said he would send others (Plu. *Pyrrh.* 26.21). The number of foreigners passing through the *agoge* may indeed have been quite substantial (cf. Cawkwell *CQ* 26 (1976) 73). Secondly the passage of Xenophon mentions bastard sons of Spartiates. These would probably be sons of Spartiate fathers and helot or slave mothers. Thirdly there would be boys of Spartiate ancestry whose families had failed to retain their citizen status, for example because they were too poor to pay their contributions to a mess (as suggested by Lotze *Historia* 11 (1962) 427-35). Lysander was probably one of these, since his father was a Spartiate descended from the Herakleidai but he was brought up in penury (Plu. *Lys.* 2.1-2); yet the alternative hypothesis that Lysander's mother was a helot or slave woman (in which case 'one of the helots' in Isok. 4.111 may be a sarcastic reference to him) cannot be ruled out. Gylippos too will have fallen into this category, but in a different way: he and his family must have been deprived of citizen status because his father Kleandridas was condemned to death for treason (Plu. *Per.* 22.3-4; cf. page 44). A fourth category may have been boys of entirely helot parentage; this possibility is suggested by the definition of mothakes as οἱ ἅμα τρεφόμενοι τοῖς υἱοῖς δοῦλοι παῖδες, 'the slave boys reared along with the sons' (Hesykhios μ 1538), and it is not excluded by the statement of Phylarkhos that the mothakes were free, since he may mean only that they became free, not that they were of free birth (cf. Cozzoli *Sesta miscellanea* 225-227).

Phylarkhos and Aelian both indicate that each mothax was the companion of a particular Spartan boy. We should assume that a boy could become a mothax only if nominated by a Spartiate father as his son's companion. Phylarkhos says that every Spartiate boy had one or more such companions, but he was writing in the second century when the number of Spartiates had become very small; mothakes were probably not as numerous as Spartiates at earlier periods.

Aelian says that mothakes who had completed the *agoge* all became citizens, and that is stated also (though without the word μόθακες) in two other texts, a fragment of Teles Περὶ φυγῆς (in Stobaios 3.40.8; cf. Mendels *Eranos* 77 (1979) 111-115) and the spurious Herakleitos *Epist.* 9.2 (*Epistolographi Graeci* ed. R. Hercher, pp. 286-7); but it conflicts with the evidence of Xenophon and Phylarkhos and should be disbelieved. We may accept from Phylarkhos that they became free men, even if their mothers were helots or slaves, and that an individual mothax could be given citizenship as a reward for outstanding service; and there is no strong reason to reject the report that Kallikratidas, Gylippos, and Lysander each attained citizenship in this way. (It is denied by Cozzoli *Sesta miscellanea* 227-31, but his argument that all three were Spartiates misses the point; there is no evidence that they were not mothakes first.)

This was the only way in which a man who was not born a Spartiate could become one. Foreigners not brought up in Sparta during boyhood could not be naturalized. Once this law was broken: Teisamenos of Elis and his brother were given Spartan citizenship because the Spartans desperately wanted his help to defeat the Persian invasion in 480/79, but 'these alone of mankind became fellow-citizens of the Spartiates' (Hdt. 9.35.1). (Instances of naturalization were alleged to have occurred in the pre-classical period, e.g. Hdt.

4.145.5, Pl. *Laws* 629a, Arist. *Pol.* 1270a 34-5. But we may take Hdt. 9.35.1 as meaning that no other instance occurred in the lifetime of Herodotos or his informants; that is preferable to emending the text, as proposed by Bicknell *Acta Classica* 25 (1982) 127-30.)

The general run of mothakes must have joined disfranchised Spartiates and liberated helots to form eventually the 'other crowd' (Plu. *Agis* 5.7) of men in Sparta who were free but not citizens. It is somewhat surprising that we do not hear more of the mothakes as a group in the fourth century, and the possibility should be considered that they became the neodamodeis. In other words, perhaps $\mu\acute{o}\theta a\xi$ was the word for a non-Spartiate boy undergoing the *agoge*, and $\nu\epsilon o\delta a\mu\acute{\omega}\delta\eta s$ for a man who had completed the *agoge* as a $\mu\acute{o}\theta a\xi$. This hypothesis has the advantage of answering two questions at once, what happened to mothakes when they grew up, and how the neodamodeis differed from helots who were simply liberated. But in problems of this kind one cannot be sure that the most economical hypothesis is the true one.

III

Military Service and the Agoge

THE INSPECTION OF INFANTS

Every Spartiate, to retain his status as one of the peers, had to perform the legal requirements (τὰ νόμιμα) to become a good soldier, as we have already seen from Xen. *LP* 3.3, 10.7 (quoted on pages 42-3). This process has been viewed by some modern writers (especially Brelich *Paides* 113-207) as an extended initiation ritual; but, whatever its origins, it is clear from Xenophon and Plutarch that by the classical period its main purpose was military efficiency.

The first of the requirements came shortly after birth. When a boy was born, the father had to take him for inspection to obtain permission to rear him.

> Plu. *Lyk.* 16.1-2. τὸ δὲ γεννηθὲν οὐκ ἦν κύριος ὁ γεννήσας τρέφειν, ἀλλ' ἔφερε λαβὼν εἰς τόπον τινὰ λέσχην καλούμενον, ἐν ᾧ καθήμενοι τῶν φυλετῶν οἱ πρεσβύτατοι καταμαθόντες τὸ παιδάριον, εἰ μὲν εὐπαγὲς εἴη καὶ ῥωμαλέον, τρέφειν ἐκέλευον, κλῆρον αὐτῷ τῶν ἐνακισχιλίων προσνείμαντες· εἰ δ' ἀγεννὲς καὶ ἄμορφον, ἀπέπεμπον εἰς τὰς λεγομένας 'Αποθέτας, παρὰ τὸ Ταΰγετον βαραθρώδη τόπον, ὡς οὔτ' αὐτῷ ζῆν ἄμεινον οὔτε τῇ πόλει τὸ μὴ καλῶς εὐθὺς ἐξ ἀρχῆς πρὸς εὐεξίαν καὶ ῥώμην πεφυκός. 'The father did not have authority to rear the baby, but he took it to a place called a *leskhe*, where the eldest members of the tribe sat and inspected

MILITARY SERVICE AND THE *AGOGE*

the child. If it was well-built and strong, they ordered him to rear it, allocating to it one of the 9,000 lots; but if it was ill-born and unshapely, they sent it away to the so-called Apothetai, a place like a pit near Taygetos, believing that it was better both for itself and for the city that it should not live if it was not well-formed for health and strength right from the start.'

Exposure of unwanted infants was a common practice throughout Greece, but outside Sparta it was normally done only on the parents' own initiative. (For comment on the significance of official intervention in the decision whether a child should be reared, see Roussel *REA* 45 (1943) 5-17.) The baby was not killed, because that would have incurred the guilt of homicide, but was left in an open place where he was likely to die from neglect. In legend (such as that of Oedipus) and in New Comedy an exposed baby was often found and reared by someone else, but in Sparta it was presumably illegal to rescue a baby from the pit called Apothetai.

The *leskhe*, where the inspection was made, was a place of resort for Spartans when not engaged in soldiering, hunting, or athletics; there were several such places with various names (Plu. *Lyk*. 25.2-3, Paus. 3.14.2, 3.15.8) and probably each tribe regularly used a particular one for its meetings. The men carrying out the inspection were the elders of the tribes. (On the tribes see pages 26-7.) No further details are given, but it is easy to imagine that the oldest members of each tribe (say those over sixty) held meetings at regular intervals (say once a month) to inspect boys brought to them, and to accept or reject them as new members of the tribe. Any boy not so inspected would be excluded from the tribe and thus from citizenship.

But Plutarch's account leaves several questions unanswered. First, Plutarch says that a father could not rear his baby without permission; but could he expose him without permission? Probably he could; if a baby was obviously weak or deformed, it seems likely that the Spartan father, like fathers elsewhere in Greece, would have exposed him at once without waiting for the elders' ruling. Secondly, did the elders only inspect the boy's physique, or did they enquire into his parentage too? Since a Spartan citizen had to have Spartiate parents, it is highly probable that the elders did satisfy themselves on this point before admitting a boy to the tribe (as at the admission of an Athenian boy to a phratry or genos, e.g. And. 1.126-7), even though there is no evidence for it. But a healthy boy found to have a non-Spartiate parent did not have to be exposed; this was a class from which some mothakes were drawn (see page 49). A third question, concerning the allocation of estates, will be discussed in connection with property (see page 94).

THE CONTROL OF BOYS

If a Spartiate boy was permitted to live, he was reared by his parents only to the age of seven, and was then taken into the system of public education, sometimes called the ἀγωγή (e.g. Plu. *Lyk.* 22.1, *Ages.* 1.2), from which only the kings' heirs were exempt (Plu. *Ages.* 1.4). From then on the boys lived together in companies. Words used for a company of boys are ἴλα, ἀγέλα, and βοῦα. (Are these three words synonyms, or do they denote different kinds of group? Hesykhios (β 865, 867) implies that a βοῦα was the same as an ἀγέλα. Comparison of Xen. *LP* 2.11, where an eiren is in charge τῆς ἴλης ἑκάστης, and Plu. *Lyk.* 17.2, where the eirens are in charge κατ' ἀγέλας, suggests that an ἀγέλα was the same as an ἴλα. For a different view see Hodkinson *Chiron* 13

(1983) 246 n. 19, but he overlooks Plu. *Lyk.* 17.2.) There were also special names for boys in particular years of their age, culminating in the name εἴρην for a young man of twenty. (For discussion of these names, see the Appendix.)

Between the ages of seven and twenty the boys underwent a harsh life and training in fighting and endurance, described by Xen. *LP* 2-3 and Plu. *Lyk.* 16-25. Those authors naturally concentrate on the most curious features, and thus make the life seem harder than perhaps it really was; yet there is no reason to reject any of their specific statements. Among other things they emphasize the small amounts of food and clothing which the boys were allowed, the hard physical exercise, and the propriety of conduct in public places. It was not just a training in the techniques of war, but was also intended to instil the virtues of αἰδώς and πειθώ (Xen. *LP* 2.2). Among the apophthegms attributed to Agesilaos are the claims that the Spartans learned from the laws of Lykourgos καταφρονεῖν τῶν ἡδονῶν and ἄρχειν τε καὶ ἄρχεσθαι, 'to despise pleasures' and 'to rule and to be ruled' (Plu. *Eth.* 210a and 212b, nos. 20 and 50-1). But we need not regard all the details of the training as being specified by law; many of them must simply have been organized by those who had charge of the boys.

So the first question of legal interest is: what persons had legal authority to give orders and punishments to the boys? The paidonomos and the eiren, according to Plu. *Lyk.* 17.2. Xenophon also mentions the paidonomos: he was appointed 'from those men from whom the highest offices are filled' (the Spartiates), and he had some young men as whip-bearers (μαστιγοφόροι) to inflict punishment when necessary (*LP* 2.2). Nothing is said about the method of his appointment; perhaps, like the ephors, a new paidonomos was elected each year, but that is a mere guess. However, the total number of

Spartiate boys at any one time before the fourth century was probably more than a thousand, and one man cannot have organized all their daily activities. So the eirens must have supervised them most of the time.

Xenophon says that Lykourgos ἔθηκε τῆς ἴλης ἑκάστης τὸν τορώτατον τῶν εἰρένων ἄρχειν, 'put the smartest of the eirens in charge of each company' (*LP* 2.11). Plutarch says αὐτοὶ προίσταντο ..., 'they themselves put in charge' the best eiren (*Lyk*. 17.2; cf. 16.8, where αὑτοῖς παρίσταντο is Madvig's conjecture). At first sight that appears to mean that the boys elected an eiren to lead them; but it would be surprising if democracy began in Sparta at the age of seven. Perhaps, instead, Plutarch means that each company had a number of eirens, who elected one of themselves to be the leader. Plutarch goes on to say that the chosen eiren commanded the boys in their fights, and organized the preparation of meals in their living quarters (*Lyk*. 17.4). In Xen. *LP* 2.5 a duty of the eiren is σῖτον συμβολεύειν, according to the text usually accepted; but the usual translation 'to contribute food' (e.g. LSJ under συμβολεύω) cannot be right, because it cannot have been the eiren's duty to supply food for the boys in his company. His duty is more likely to have been distribution than contribution, and συμβολεύειν (a verb which is found nowhere else) probably needs emendation.

But the paidonomos and the eirens were not the only persons having authority over the boys.

> Xen. *LP* 2.10. ὅπως δὲ μηδ' εἰ ὁ παιδονόμος ἀπέλθοι, ἔρημοί ποτε οἱ παῖδες εἶεν ἄρχοντος, ἐποίησε τὸν ἀεὶ παρόντα τῶν πολιτῶν κύριον εἶναι καὶ ἐπιτάττειν τοῖς παισὶν ὅ τι [ἂν] ἀγαθὸν δοκοίη εἶναι, καὶ κολάζειν, εἴ τι ἁμαρτάνοιεν. 'In order that, even if the paidonomos went away, the boys might never be without a ruler, he

MILITARY SERVICE AND THE *AGOGE*

(Lykourgos) gave authority to any citizen who was present on any occasion to give the boys whatever order he thought fit, and to punish them if they did anything wrong.'

Xenophon mentions again later that every Spartan man rules (ἄρχειν means authority to give orders and punishments) other men's sons as well as his own (*LP* 6.1-2). He makes it sound like a matter of chance whether any man happened to be present on any particular occasion to take charge of a group of boys. But Plutarch in another passage hints at a more systematic arrangement.

> Plu. *Lyk.* 18.6-7. πολλάκις δὲ καὶ πρεσβυτέρων παρόντων καὶ ἀρχόντων ὁ εἴρην ἐκόλαζε τοὺς παῖδας, ἀπόδειξιν διδοὺς εἰ μετὰ λόγου καὶ ὡς δεῖ κολάζει. καὶ κολάζων μὲν οὐκ ἐκωλύετο, τῶν δὲ παίδων ἀπελθόντων εὐθύνας ὑπεῖχεν, εἰ τραχύτερον τοῦ δέοντος ἐπετίμησεν, ἢ τοὐναντίον ἐκλελυμένως καὶ ἀτόνως. 'Frequently, even when older men were present and in charge, the eiren used to punish the boys, showing whether he punished reasonably and properly. While inflicting the punishment he was not stopped, but after the boys had gone away he underwent examination to see if he had imposed a harsher penalty than he ought, or on the contrary a lax and careless one.'

And a few lines later Plutarch mentions οἱ ἄρχοντες again (*Lyk.* 18.8). So it appears that the boys were regularly supervised by adults (men over thirty), and the eirens' authority was limited (though, in the last passage quoted, it is interesting to note how the older men took care not to undermine an eiren's authority, and refrained from criticizing him in the boys' presence). Perhaps it was normal for the paidonomos to get, by informal means, a number of other men to assist him; and these may have been the men who were called ἄμπαιδες, a word which Hesykhios defines as meaning οἱ τῶν παίδων ἐπιμελούμενοι παρὰ Λάκωσιν, 'those in charge of the boys, among the Lakonians' (α 3769).

No text specifies any legal restriction on the penalties which eirens could impose, but surely only certain kinds of penalty were sanctioned by convention. Plutarch mentions πληγαὶ καὶ τὸ πεινῆν, 'blows and hunger' (*Lyk.* 17.6), and those may well have been the two most usual kinds of punishment for boys. In another passage we read of a boy getting a bite in the thumb from the eiren (*Lyk.* 18.5; for conjectures about the origin of this penalty see den Boer *Laconian Studies* 274-81). Isokrates mentions ἀργύριον ἀποτίνειν, 'paying money' (12.212); but since the importance of money was minimized in Sparta, and the private possession of silver (which is what ἀργύριον should strictly mean) was for some time actually illegal (see page 119), it is unlikely that boys were allowed to have money, and probably Isokrates has made a mistake. The ultimate penalty for a boy who flinched from the demands made on him was exclusion from citizenship (Xen. *LP* 3.3, 10.7), but so serious a penalty could presumably not be imposed by an eiren; it would need the authority of the paidonomos at least, and probably of the ephors.

But despite the authority given to others, a father was still regarded as having the primary responsibility for keeping his sons in order, if we may believe one of the anonymous apophthegms: 'When brothers disputed with one another, they punished the father for allowing his sons to quarrel' (Plu. *Eth.* 233f). That is probably a reference to a particular incident rather than a law, but it does imply that a father's legal authority over his son was not wholly transferred to the community.

MILITARY SERVICE AND THE *AGOGE*

THEFT BY BOYS

From the legal point of view, one of the most interesting aspects of the *agoge* is the treatment of theft.

> Xen. *LP* 2.6-8. ὡς δὲ μὴ ὑπὸ λιμοῦ ἄγαν αὖ πιέζοιντο, ἀπραγμόνως μὲν αὐτοῖς οὐκ ἔδωκε λαμβάνειν ὧν ἂν προσδέωνται, κλέπτειν δ' ἐφῆκεν ἔστιν ἃ τῷ λιμῷ ἐπικουροῦντας.... ταῦτα οὖν δὴ πάντα δῆλον ὅτι μηχανικωτέρους τῶν ἐπιτηδείων βουλόμενος τοὺς παῖδας ποιεῖν καὶ πολεμικωτέρους οὕτως ἐπαίδευσεν. εἴποι δ' ἂν οὖν τις, τί δῆτα, εἴπερ τὸ κλέπτειν ἀγαθὸν ἐνόμιζε, πολλὰς πληγὰς ἐπέβαλλε τῷ ἁλισκομένῳ; ὅτι, φημὶ ἐγώ, καὶ τἆλλα, ὅσα ἄνθρωποι διδάσκουσι, κολάζουσι τὸν μὴ καλῶς ὑπηρετοῦντα. κἀκεῖνοι οὖν τοὺς ἁλισκομένους ὡς κακῶς κλέπτοντας τιμωροῦνται. 'On the other hand, so that they might not be too much oppressed by hunger, though he (Lykourgos) did not allow them to take whatever they needed without trouble, he permitted them to steal some things to relieve their hunger.... So clearly he educated the boys in this way because he wished to make them more resourceful at obtaining supplies, and more warlike. Why then, you might ask, if he thought theft a good thing, did he impose a severe beating on a boy who was caught? Because, I reply, just as in all the other lessons which people teach they punish the person who does not perform well, so too in this case they punish those who are caught on the ground that they steal badly.'

The phrase ἔστιν ἅ, 'some things', should be noted. In another place Xenophon says more clearly that the boys were encouraged to steal ὅσα μὴ κωλύει νόμος, 'all that is not forbidden by law' (*An.* 4.6.14). This shows that the law made clear what kinds of thing boys were not permitted to take.

Plutarch's account of this matter agrees essentially with Xenophon's (*Lyk.* 17.5-6). Isokrates in his Panathenaic speech comments on the practice with disapproval.

> Isok. 12.211-12. ἐκεῖνοι γὰρ καθ' ἑκάστην τὴν ἡμέραν εὐθὺς ἐξ εὐνῆς ἐκπέμπουσι τοὺς παῖδας, μεθ' ὧν ἂν ἕκαστοι βουληθῶσιν, λόγῳ μὲν ἐπὶ θήραν, ἔργῳ δ' ἐπὶ κλωπείαν τῶν ἐν τοῖς ἀγροῖς κατοικούντων· ἐν ᾗ συμβαίνει τοὺς μὲν ληφθέντας ἀργύριον ἀποτίνειν καὶ πληγὰς λαμβάνειν, τοὺς δὲ πλεῖστα κακουργήσαντας καὶ λαθεῖν δυνηθέντας ἔν τε τοῖς παισὶν εὐδοκιμεῖν μᾶλλον τῶν ἄλλων, ἐπειδὰν δ' εἰς ἄνδρας συντελῶσιν, ἢν ἐμμείνωσιν τοῖς ἤθεσιν οἷς παῖδες ὄντες ἐμελέτησαν, ἐγγὺς εἶναι τῶν μεγίστων ἀρχῶν. 'The Spartans send out their boys every day, as soon as they get up, with whatever companions they each wish, allegedly to hunt, but in fact to steal from those who live in the country. The practice is that those who are caught are fined and beaten, but those who do most wrong and are able to escape detection have a higher reputation among the boys, and when they come to man's estate, if they keep to the habits which they adopted as boys, are in line for the highest offices.'

Isokrates is making a rhetorical point, not a historical record, and one may hesitate to trust his words in details. The reference to punishment by a monetary fine is probably wrong (see page 58). The phrase τῶν ἐν τοῖς ἀγροῖς κατοικούντων, if interpreted strictly, means that theft from perioikoi and helots only was permitted, since all Spartiates resided in the city; but Spartiates owned land in the country, on which helots resided, and it is unlikely that the boys were expected to enquire who was the legal owner of an orchard before they stole the apples. Besides, Plutarch mentions that some of the boys stole food from the Spartiate men's messes (*Lyk*. 17.5), which shows that they did not steal only from perioikoi. So Isokrates adds little trustworthy information to Xenophon. Both say that the Spartans approved of theft by boys, but punished those who were caught. The difference between this and other people's attitude to theft may seem to be purely theoretical; in any case thieves are punished if they are caught, and are not punished if they are not caught. But in fact there is a significant difference, and Isokrates's account points to it: his main purpose is to emphasize that in Sparta a boy who stole without being caught was respected by the other boys, and later by the citizens generally. The theft, in other words, was known at the time to all the boys, and later to everyone, and yet the thief was not punished. Thus in this context 'to be caught' (ἁλίσκεσθαι), so as to incur punishment, cannot mean merely to be known by other people to have stolen; it must mean to be caught in the act by the owner of the produce being stolen. The conclusion should be that theft of food by boys was permitted, and they were punished only if the owner of the food caught them in the act, not if the theft was detected by someone else or at a later time.

HOMOSEXUALITY

Another question about the conduct of boys is whether homosexual relationships and acts were permitted or regulated by law. Plutarch seems to take for granted that boys had lovers (*Lyk*. 17.1, 18.8), and even that young men up to the age of thirty had lovers over that age (*Lyk*. 25.1). Xenophon shows a greater inclination to argue on the subject. He mentions practices in other parts of Greece, and proceeds to contrast with them what Lykourgos did in Sparta.

Xen. *LP* 2.13-14. ὁ δὲ Λυκοῦργος ἐναντία καὶ τούτοις πᾶσι γνούς, εἰ μέν τις αὐτὸς ὢν οἷον δεῖ ἀγασθεὶς ψυχὴν παιδὸς πειρῶτο ἄμεμπτον φίλον ἀποτελέσασθαι καὶ συνεῖναι, ἐπῄνει καὶ καλλίστην παιδείαν ταύτην ἐνόμιζεν· εἰ δέ τις παιδὸς σώματος ὀρεγόμενος φανείη, αἴσχιστον τοῦτο θεὶς ἐποίησεν ἐν Λακεδαίμονι μηδὲν ἧττον ἐραστὰς παιδικῶν ἀπέχεσθαι ἢ γονεῖς παίδων ἢ καὶ ἀδελφοὶ ἀδελφῶν εἰς ἀφροδίσια ἀπέχονται. τὸ μέντοι ταῦτα ἀπιστεῖσθαι ὑπό τινων οὐ θαυμάζω· ἐν πολλαῖς γὰρ τῶν πόλεων οἱ νόμοι οὐκ ἐναντιοῦνται ταῖς πρὸς τοὺς παῖδας ἐπιθυμίαις. 'Lykourgos's view was the reverse of all these. If someone, who himself was what a man ought to be, admired a boy's character and attempted to make him a blameless friend and to associate with him, he approved of that and considered it an excellent kind of education. But if someone obviously desired a boy's body, he counted that disgraceful and he caused lovers to keep away from boys in Sparta just as much as parents keep away from children and brothers from sisters for sexual purposes. However, I am not surprised that some people disbelieve this; for in many cities the laws do not oppose desire with regard to boys.'

Xenophon says that Lykourgos disapproved of physical homosexual relationships. But he does not say that Lykourgos gave an order (though elsewhere in the book ἔταξε is common), and while he refers vaguely to 'the laws' of other cities, he seems unable to point to a Spartan law. Instead he claims that Lykourgos changed the Spartans' moral opinion on the subject, and then he reveals that he does not expect all his readers to believe even that. It is clear that he is idealizing here: he attributes to Lykourgos what he believes ought to be the rule but in fact is not. We may conclude that there was no law banning homosexual acts with boys in Sparta. Nevertheless we can accept that moral relationships between boys and

MILITARY SERVICE AND THE *AGOGE*

lovers were of greater significance and interest than physical ones, and proceed to consider whether such moral relationships were subject to legal regulation.

Plu. *Lyk.* 18.8. ἐκοινώνουν δ' οἱ ἐρασταὶ τοῖς παισὶ τῆς δόξης ἐπ' ἀμφότερα· καὶ λέγεταί ποτε παιδὸς ἐν τῷ μάχεσθαι φωνὴν ἀγεννῆ προεμένου, ζημιωθῆναι τὸν ἐραστὴν ὑπὸ τῶν ἀρχόντων. 'The lovers shared the boys' reputations, both good and bad. It is said that on one occasion, when a boy in fighting let out an ignoble squeal, his lover was punished by the men in charge.'

Ael. *Var. Hist.* 3.10. ὅτε τις τῶν παρ' αὐτοῖς καλῶν πλούσιον ἐραστὴν προείλετο τοῦ χρηστοῦ πένητος, ἐπέβαλον αὐτῷ χρήματα, κολάζοντες ὡς ἔοικε τὴν φιλοχρηματίαν τῇ τῶν χρημάτων ζημίᾳ. ἄλλον δέ τινα ἄνδρα καλὸν κἀγαθὸν οὐδενὸς ἐρῶντα τῶν καλῶς πεφυκότων καὶ τοῦτον ἐζημίωσαν, ὅτι χρηστὸς ὢν οὐδενὸς ἤρα· δῆλον γὰρ ὡς ὅμοιον ἂν ἑαυτῷ κἀκεῖνον ἀπέφηνεν, ἴσως δ' ἂν καὶ ἄλλον. δεινὴ γὰρ ἡ τῶν ἐραστῶν πρὸς τὰ παιδικὰ εὔνοια ἀρετὰς ἐνεργάσασθαι, ὅταν αὐτοὶ σεμνοὶ ὦσιν· ἐπεί τοι Λακωνικὸς καὶ οὗτος νόμος, ὅταν ἁμάρτῃ μειράκιον, τῇ μὲν ἀφελείᾳ τοῦ τρόπου καὶ τῷ νεαρῷ τῆς ἡλικίας συγγινώσκουσι, τὸν δὲ ἐραστὴν ὑπὲρ αὐτοῦ κολάζουσιν, ἐπιγνώμονας αὐτοὺς καὶ ἐξεταστὰς ὧν ἐκεῖνοι πράττουσι κελεύοντες εἶναι. 'When a handsome boy there preferred a rich lover to a worthy but poor one, they (the ephors) imposed a fine on him, apparently punishing desire for money by a monetary penalty. Another fine gentleman, who did not love any of the handsome boys, was also fined by them because although he was good he did not love anyone; for evidently he would have made that boy, and perhaps another too, similar in character to himself. For the favour of lovers to boys is effective at implanting good qualities, as long as the lovers themselves are respectable. And in fact this is also a Lakonian law: when a lad does wrong, they forgive his callowness and youthfulness and punish his lover instead, because they order the lovers to inspect and appraise the boys' behaviour.'

Plutarch seems to imply, and Aelian states explicitly, that lovers had some legal responsibility for boys' conduct. In the light of these passages we should look again at Xen. *LP* 3.3 (quoted on pages 42-3), where we read that Lykourgos arranged for 'those personally connected with them' (τοὺς κηδομένους) to supervise the youths. The verb κήδομαι can refer to the affection of a lover (cf. Pl. *Symp.* 210c). So Xenophon too might be interpreted as meaning that it was normal, or even compulsory, for men and boys to form relationships, in which the man was required to be the boy's moral tutor.

The law that the lover was punished if the boy misbehaved, if genuine, shows a very unusual and interesting kind of vicarious accountability. In many other societies, ancient and modern, a child's parents may be held responsible for his offence; but in Sparta the lover appears to have been almost *in loco parentis*. But is this law genuine? Plutarch's words λέγεταί ποτε show that he is not aware of a law making the lover accountable for the boy's conduct; he is just repeating an anecdote which he has heard about one incident, and does not vouch for the truth even of that. And surely Xenophon, in his efforts to justify Spartan homosexuality (*LP* 2.13-14), would have mentioned this law explicitly if it had existed in his time. Therefore it is best to reject Aelian's statement about the law; Aelian probably read, either in Plutarch or more likely in some other source now lost, the anecdote which Plutarch relates about one unusual incident, and misinterpreted it as referring to an established rule. Furthermore the rest of this paragraph of Aelian may also be regarded with suspicion. The anecdote about the boy fined for giving preference to a rich lover is suspect because it is unlikely that a boy would have money to pay a fine; it may be a moralist's tale suggested by the incident concerning the daughters of Lysander and their suitors (see page 73). The second anecdote, about a good man fined for failure to love a boy, is even harder to believe. So this whole passage of Aelian should be dismissed as untrustworthy. Nor should the passage of Plutarch be treated as firm evidence, in view of the cautious λέγεται: if the ephors did indeed punish a lover on some occasion, they may have had some other reason besides the one which Plutarch gives. And Xenophon's phrase τοὺς κηδομένους may after all refer to fathers and brothers rather than lovers.

Altogether, then, the preferable conclusion is that the Spartans had no law on the subject of homosexual relationships. One of the best recent writers on Spartan society claims that 'the evidence of Xenophon and Plutarch is sufficient to establish the important conclusion that pederasty in Sparta was institutionalised' (Cartledge *PCPS* 207 (1981) 22). But the language of Xen. *LP* 2.13-14 does not suggest an institution. On the contrary, 'if someone... admired a boy's character..., (Lykourgos) approved of that' implies that only some boys inspired love, and that this might happen at any time. This wording is quite inappropriate for a system in which every boy on reaching a certain age was allocated to a lover; and it is incredible that, if such a system had existed in Sparta, Xenophon and Plutarch would have refrained from saying so.

YOUNG MEN

Spartiates between the ages of twenty and thirty were those variously called οἱ ἡβῶντες or τὰ δέκα ἀφ' ἥβης or εἴρενες (see pages 164-7). They were no longer boys, and yet they were still not full citizens. They were allowed to grow their hair long (Xen. *LP* 11.3, Plu. *Lyk.* 22.2); yet they still slept in a central dormitory, not at home (Plu. *Lyk.* 15.7), and they did not do their own shopping (Plu. *Lyk.* 25.1, quoted on page 160). They were not allowed to hold office (Xen. *LP* 4.7). There is no evidence to show whether they could attend meetings of the assembly of citizens; in view of the other restrictions on them, I suppose that they could not.

An eiren who was selected to lead a company of boys (Xen. *LP* 2.11, Plu. *Lyk.* 17.2) must have devoted most of his time to that. Presumably he was exempt from military service, since the boys could not be abandoned in wartime. Otherwise men of this age were liable to military service; indeed τὰ δέκα ἀφ' ἥβης were probably the most active part of the army. Xenophon also recounts a further process of selection within it.

> Xen. *LP* 4.3-6. αἱροῦνται τοίνυν αὐτῶν οἱ ἔφοροι ἐκ τῶν ἀκμαζόντων τρεῖς ἄνδρας· οὗτοι δὲ ἱππαγρέται καλοῦνται. τούτων δ' ἕκαστος ἄνδρας ἑκατὸν καταλέγει, διασαφηνίζων ὅτου ἕνεκα τοὺς μὲν προτιμᾷ, τοὺς δὲ ἀποδοκιμάζει. οἱ οὖν μὴ τυγχάνοντες τῶν καλῶν πολεμοῦσι τοῖς τε ἀποστείλασιν αὐτοὺς καὶ τοῖς αἱρεθεῖσιν ἀνθ' αὑτῶν καὶ παραφυλάττουσιν ἀλλήλους, ἐάν τι παρὰ τὰ καλὰ νομιζόμενα ῥᾳδιουργῶσι. ... καὶ γὰρ πυκτεύουσι διὰ τὴν ἔριν ὅπου ἂν συμβάλωσι· διαλύειν μέντοι τοὺς μαχομένους πᾶς ὁ παραγενόμενος κύριος. ἢν δέ τις ἀπειθῇ τῷ διαλύοντι, ἄγει αὐτὸν ὁ παιδονόμος ἐπὶ τοὺς ἐφόρους· οἱ δὲ ζημιοῦσι μεγαλείως, καθιστάναι βου-

λόμενοι εἰς τὸ μήποτε ὀργὴν τοῦ μὴ πείθεσθαι τοῖς νόμοις κρατῆσαι. 'The ephors select three of them, out of those in their prime; these are called *hippagretai*. Each of these enrols a hundred men, making clear his reason for preferring them and rejecting the others. Those who fail to gain the honour make war both on the men who turned them away and on those selected in preference to them, and they keep an eye on one another, to watch for any lapse from the code of honour.... Because of the rivalry they also spar wherever they meet, but any passer-by has authority to break up the fight. Anyone who disobeys the order to break it up is taken by the paidonomos to the ephors, and the ephors punish him heavily, in order to teach him never to let anger get the better of obedience to the laws.'

The three hippagretai, who picked the rest of the three hundred, themselves belonged to the twenty-to-thirty age-group, as αὐτῶν shows; the meaning of ἀκμαζόντων is probably that they were in the final year of that period. The three hundred whom they selected formed the *corps d'élite* of the Spartan army. In the fifth century they were known as the ἱππεῖς, 'cavalry' (Hdt. 8.124.3, Thuc. 5.72.4), and presumably they had in earlier times been mounted, although in the classical period they did not in fact have horses (Str. 10.4.18). For most of the fifth century the Spartans did not have any mounted soldiers (Thuc. 4.55.2). But in the fourth century they did, and the term ἱππεῖς was used for those (Xen. *LP* 11.2, *Hell.* 6.4.10), not for the special corps of young men, which came to be called simply 'the three hundred' (Plu. *Lyk.* 25.6).

Two points of legal interest emerge from Xenophon's account of this corps. The first is that any passer-by (but surely this only means any Spartiate) had authority to tell two young men to stop fighting, and his order had the force of a legal interdict; they were not punished for fighting, but only for continuing to fight after someone told them to stop. The second is the position of the paidonomos in relation to the young men. He was concerned with them, as well as with boys; yet he could not simply punish them, as he punished boys, but had to take them before the ephors for judgement. This illustrates the ambivalent status of young men between twenty and thirty.

ADULT MEN

A Spartiate remained liable to military service until he was sixty, forty years after coming of age (τετταράκοντα ἀφ᾽ ἥβης, Xen. *Hell.* 5.4.13, Plu. *Ages.* 24.3). Throughout that time he had to take exercise and keep fit and alert.

    Xen. *LP* 5.7. οὐδὲ γὰρ ὑπὸ φανοῦ τὸν ἔτι ἔμφρουρον ἔξεστι πορεύεσθαι. 'Nor is it permitted for a man still liable to military service to travel with a light.'

    Xen. *LP* 5.8. ἐπέταξε τὸν ἀεὶ πρεσβύτατον ἐν τῷ γυμνασίῳ ἑκάστῳ ἐπιμελεῖσθαι ὡς μήποτε †αὑτοὶ ἐλάττους τῶν σιτίων γίγνεσθαι†. 'He (Lykourgos) instructed that the oldest man in each gymnasium should ensure that they never...' (The text is corrupt. H. Schenkl's conjecture is good, though not certain: ὡς μήποτε ἀγυμνάστους τῶν σιτίων γεύεσθαι, 'that they never eat their food without first taking exercise'.)

    Xen. *LP* 12.5. καὶ γυμνάζεσθαι δὲ προαγορεύεται ὑπὸ τοῦ νόμου ἅπασι Λακεδαιμονίοις, ἔωσπερ ἂν στρατεύωνται. 'Gymnastics are also prescribed by law for all Lakedaimonians, as long as they perform military service.'

MILITARY SERVICE AND THE *AGOGE*

The purpose of the law forbidding the use of a light when walking in the dark was evidently to ensure that a man would remain capable of a high standard of alertness. Gymnastics, it is clear from *LP* 12.5, were required by law, but it is surprising to read in *LP* 5.8 that this law was to be enforced by 'the oldest man in each gymnasium'. This would work only if every man was required to attend a gymnasium; but if membership of a gymnasium was compulsory, like membership of a mess (see pages 111-12), one would expect Xenophon and Plutarch to have mentioned that. Elsewhere γυμνάσιον sometimes means simply a group of men who meet regularly (e.g. Ar. *Wasps* 527), and I suggest that Xenophon here uses the word to refer to membership of a mess, which was compulsory for Spartiates. If Schenkl's emendation is correct, it is easy to see how the senior man in each mess could ensure that none of the other members sat down to dinner without first taking exercise.

Persistent failure to keep fit would make a Spartiate liable to lose his citizenship, in accordance with the principle stated in Xen. *LP* 10.7 (quoted on page 43). Only after his sixtieth year could he relax with impunity.

The organization of the Spartan army is a complex subject which will not be considered in this book. For the most part it was a matter of military practice rather than law. However, it is appropriate to note here two Spartan laws on military subjects which are mentioned by the Attic orator Lykourgos in his speech against Leokrates. First, a law about the inspiring war poems of Tyrtaios. Sparta is perhaps the only state ever to have made listening to poetry compulsory.

> Lyk. *Leo.* 107. νόμον ἔθεντο, ὅταν ἐν τοῖς ὅπλοις ἐξεστρατευμένοι ὦσι, καλεῖν ἐπὶ τὴν τοῦ βασιλέως σκηνὴν ἀκουσομένους τῶν Τυρταίου ποιημάτων

ἅπαντας, νομίζοντες οὕτως ἂν αὐτοὺς μάλιστα πρὸ τῆς πατρίδος ἐθέλειν ἀποθνῄσκειν. 'They made a law that, whenever they were out on an armed campaign, they should all be summoned to the king's tent to hear the poems of Tyrtaios, because they thought that in this way they would be most ready to die for their country.'

Later Lykourgos mentions a law specifying death as the penalty for desertion.

> Lyk. *Leo.* 129. νόμον γὰρ ἔθεντο περὶ ἁπάντων τῶν μὴ θελόντων ὑπὲρ τῆς πατρίδος κινδυνεύειν, διαρρήδην λέγοντα ἀποθνῄσκειν. 'They made a law about all who declined to face danger on behalf of their country, saying explicitly that they were to die.'

He continues for several sentences praising this law, and has the text of it read out to the Athenian jury. The text is unfortunately not preserved, but it must have confirmed his statement of what the law said. There is also a corrupt sentence in Arist. *Pol.* 1285a 7-10 (quoted on page 125) which implies that the king could execute on the spot a deserter in battle. We should therefore accept that the death penalty was prescribed for desertion. Yet there is other evidence that the penalty for cowardice was disfranchisement (see pages 44-6). How cowardice deserving death was distinguished from cowardice deserving merely disfranchisement, no one tells us. It may be that no distinction was laid down and it was simply left to the discretion of the king to execute if he thought fit in the heat of a battle.

IV

Women and Marriage

THE UPBRINGING OF GIRLS

Women could not become soldiers; their principal function in the system attributed to Lykourgos was to produce sons who would be the soldiers of the next generation. Although girls were not subjected to the severe upbringing which boys underwent, and always lived at home rather than in a state-organized place of residence, steps were taken to ensure that they were physically fit for child-bearing. (The best modern study of the life of Spartan women is Cartledge's article in *CQ* 31 (1981) 84-105.)

It is not known whether girls, like boys, had to be inspected soon after birth for permission to rear them to be obtained. Plu. *Lyk*. 16.1-2 (quoted on pages 52-3), describing the procedure for inspection, uses neuter words for the child (τὸ γεννηθέν, τὸ παιδάριον) which might refer to either sex. But the reference to allocation of a lot (κλῆρος) indicates that the passage was written with boys in mind, and was not intended to be taken as a statement about girls. Thus it is possible that the decision whether to rear a girl was left entirely to the parents.

Girls were required by 'the laws of Lykourgos' to exercise their bodies (Xen. *LP* 1.4). We are told of girls' contests in running, wrestling, and throwing the discus and javelin, and also of religious occasions, with processions, dancing, and singing, in which girls took part in the nude (Plu. *Lyk*. 14.

3-7). But it is not clear how far those activities should be regarded as legal requirements, in the sense that girls would be punished if they did not participate.

In Athenian comedy a Spartan woman is presented as a superb physical specimen strong enough to strangle a bull (Ar. *Lys.* 78-84). So it is surprising that Aristotle criticizes Spartan law for allowing the women, by contrast with the men, to live dissolutely and luxuriously; he reports a tradition that Lykourgos gave up an attempt to bring the women under legal control (*Pol.* 1269b 19-23, 1270a 6-8). Perhaps the best way of reconciling these statements with the other evidence is to assume that women were no longer required to continue taking exercise after they had borne children, or after they had passed child-bearing age.

THE AGE FOR MARRIAGE

According to Xenophon, Lykourgos ordained that marriages should take place at the best age for child-bearing.

> Xen. *LP* 1.6. ἀποπαύσας τοῦ ὁπότε βούλοιντο ἕκαστοι γυναῖκα ἄγεσθαι, ἔταξεν ἐν ἀκμαῖς τῶν σωμάτων τοὺς γάμους ποιεῖσθαι, καὶ τοῦτο συμφέρον τῇ εὐγονίᾳ νομίζων. 'He stopped men from marrying a wife at whatever time each of them wished, and ordained that marriages should be made at the prime of physical development, considering this also to be beneficial to the birth of good children.'

Before this passage (in 1.3-4) Xenophon has been discussing the nourishment and exercise which women need if they are to bear good children; and immediately after it (in 1.7) he turns to the arrangement made by Lykourgos for old men who had young wives. Thus the context makes it likely that

WOMEN AND MARRIAGE

here he means that a marriage had to take place when the woman had reached a good age for child-bearing, and is not saying that there was any restriction on the age of the man. This interpretation is strengthened by Plutarch's remark that the Spartans used to marry 'not little girls or ones unripe for marriage, but in their prime and mature' (*Lyk.* 15.4, quoted on page 78). Elsewhere in Greece women were married at the age of fourteen (Xen. *Oik.* 7.5) or even twelve (*Law of Gortyn* 12.17-19). Since neither Xenophon nor Plutarch mentions a specific age, probably the Spartan law was simply that the woman must be fully developed physically.

But even if it is correct that Xen. *LP* 1.6 refers to the age of women only, there is other evidence that the law encouraged men to marry before reaching a certain age. (For women, there is evidence only for a minimum age; for men, only for a maximum age. In the third century the future Kleomenes III was married while still a boy and 'not really old enough for marriage' (Plu. *Kleom.* 1.1). This means that his marriage was inappropriate physically, but not invalid legally; the contrary interpretation assumed by Cartledge *CQ* 31 (1981) 94 is incorrect.) Plutarch relates that after the death of Lysander some suitors of his daughters, discovering from the examination of his affairs that he was not rich, as they had supposed, but poor, gave up their suits for the daughters, and were punished for doing so. He then attempts to say what the law on this subject was.

> Plu. *Lys.* 30.7. ἦν γὰρ ὡς ἔοικεν ἐν Σπάρτῃ καὶ ἀγαμίου δίκη καὶ ὀψιγαμίου καὶ κακογαμίου· ταύτῃ δ' ὑπῆγον μάλιστα τοὺς ἀντὶ τῶν ἀγαθῶν καὶ οἰκείων τοῖς πλουσίοις κηδεύοντας. 'There was, it appears, in Sparta a legal action for not marrying and for marrying late and for marrying badly. Subject to this were in particular

those who allied themselves to rich men instead of good men and relatives.'

The phrase ὡς ἔοικεν shows that Plutarch himself is uncertain here. Failure to marry a daughter of Lysander would not by itself amount to any of the three offences listed; the men punished must each have committed one or other of those offences in addition. ἀγάμιον is simply not marrying at all. But clearly a young man would not be held guilty of this offence; there must have been some specific age by which men were expected to marry, and after which they were guilty of ἀγάμιον if they did not, but there is no evidence to show what age it was. ὀψιγάμιον is marrying late; probably that means after the age at which a man became guilty of ἀγάμιον if he remained unmarried. One might think 'Better late than never'; but the Spartans probably considered that an older husband was less likely to beget children, and by excluding a younger man he was diminishing a woman's output. κακογάμιον, marrying badly, presumably meant marrying the daughter of a man who either had committed some offence or was not a Spartiate. It is hard to believe that a father-in-law's wealth made his son-in-law guilty of κακογάμιον, as Plutarch seems to have thought; however, it is possible that the ephors were free to decide what made a marriage bad, and that they did include wealth and poverty among the circumstances which they took into account in the particular case of the suitors of the daughters of Lysander.

It is not known what penalties were imposed for marrying late or marrying badly; but they did not include dissolution of the marriage, for we read elsewhere about arrangements which could be made when an old man had a young wife (Xen. *LP* 1.7, Plu. *Lyk*. 15.12, both quoted on pages 83-5). For not marrying, Xen. *LP* 9.5 mentions a penalty without saying what it was, but information about penalties is given by another passage of Plutarch.

> Plu. *Lyk.* 15.1-3. καὶ ἀτιμίαν τινὰ προσέθηκε τοῖς ἀγάμοις. εἴργοντο γὰρ ἐν ταῖς γυμνοπαιδίαις τῆς θέας· τοῦ δὲ χειμῶνος οἱ μὲν ἄρχοντες αὐτοὺς ἐκέλευον ἐν κύκλῳ γυμνοὺς περιιέναι τὴν ἀγοράν, οἱ δὲ περιιόντες ᾖδον εἰς αὐτοὺς ᾠδήν τινα πεποιημένην ὡς δίκαια πάσχοιεν ὅτι τοῖς νόμοις ἀπειθοῦσι. τιμῆς δὲ καὶ θεραπείας ἣν νέοι πρεσβυτέροις παρεῖχον ἐστέρηντο· ὅθεν καὶ τὸ πρὸς Δερκυλλίδαν ῥηθὲν οὐδεὶς ἐμέμψατο, καίπερ εὐδόκιμον ὄντα στρατηγόν. ἐπιόντι γὰρ αὐτῷ τῶν νεωτέρων τις ἕδρας οὐχ ὑπεῖξεν [αὐτῷ] εἰπών "οὐδὲ γὰρ ἐμοὶ σὺ τὸν ὑπείξοντα γεγέννηκας". 'He also attached some dishonour to unmarried men. They were excluded from watching at the Gymnopaidiai; and in winter the authorities used to order them to walk round the Agora in a circle, undressed, and as they walked round they sang a song composed against themselves, that they were being justly treated for disobeying the laws. They were deprived of the honour and attendance which young men gave to older ones. That was why no one found fault with the remark which was made to Derkyllidas, although he was a distinguished general: one of the younger men did not give up a seat to him when he approached, and said "You haven't produced a son who will give up a seat to me".'

The Gymnopaidiai were a festival held in the heat of the summer (cf. Pl. *Laws* 633c) at which, as the name implies, boys competed in the nude; thus the ban on unmarried spectators may have been intended to discourage homosexuality in older men. (For an alternative explanation in terms of religion and magic, see den Boer *Laconian Studies* 221-6.) The other penalties may have been less formal and regular. 'The authorities used to order them . . .' seems to imply that the humiliating walk round the Agora did not take place unless some official took the initiative; it may be that this happened only on a few occasions, not every year. And, if an unmarried man was willing to tolerate these public slights, he did not suffer further legal disabilities; that is clear from the anecdote about Derkyllidas, who, though unmarried, was able to become a general. Perhaps celibacy suffered less disapproval at some periods than at others. Plutarch attributes the penalties, like so much else, to Lykourgos, and there is no strong reason to date them as late as 500 or 490 (as suggested by Daube *PCA* 74 (1977) 14, Cartledge *Sparta* 309-10).

Besides the penalties for celibacy, there were also rewards for producing children.

> Arist. *Pol.* 1270b 1-4. βουλόμενος γὰρ ὁ νομοθέτης ὡς πλείστους εἶναι τοὺς Σπαρτιάτας, προάγεται τοὺς πολίτας ὅτι πλείστους ποιεῖσθαι παῖδας· ἔστι γὰρ αὐτοῖς νόμος τὸν μὲν γεννήσαντα τρεῖς υἱοὺς ἄφρουρον εἶναι, τὸν δὲ τέτταρας ἀτελῆ πάντων. 'Wishing that the Spartiates should be as many as possible, the legislator encourages the citizens to produce as many children as possible; for they have a law that a man who has begotten three sons is to be exempt from military service, and one who has begotten four is to be exempt from all contributions.'

The sense of ἄφρουρος is probably exemption from all military service, not merely from routine guard duties, for at Sparta the word φρουρά was used of campaigns abroad (Xen. *LP* 13.11, *Hell.* 2.4.29); ἀτελὴς πάντων includes exemption both from military service and from taxation. Aelian gives the same information, except that he says that five sons were needed to secure the second privilege (*Var. Hist.* 6.6); either he or, less probably, Aristotle has got the number wrong. Neither author tells us whether the exemptions took effect as soon as the sons had been born, or not until they had reached military age; but even in the latter case they were very substantial privileges.

MARRIAGE PROCEDURE

Most Spartans, then, probably did marry. How was a legal marriage made? In Greece generally, as far as we know, it was normal for a father to give his daughter to a husband; a marriage was an arrangement made by agreement between the father and the bridegroom, in which the woman herself did not necessarily have any say. In Athens the formula of betrothal (ἐγγύη) pronounced by the father, or by the nearest surviving male relative, was a prerequisite, without which a marriage was not valid. Was this true also in Sparta? (This question is not satisfactorily answered by Cartledge *CQ* 31 (1981) 99-100. He treats Xen. *LP* 9.5 as decisive; but the key word 'ask' is implanted by Cartledge and is not in the text of Xenophon.) Betrothal seems to be implied by a passage of Herodotos in which we read that Arkhidamos married Lampito, daughter of Leotykhidas, δόντος αὐτῷ Λευτυχίδεω, 'Leotykhidas giving her to him' (6.71.2). And in another passage Herodotos remarks that the kings decide who is to marry an heiress ἢν μή περ ὁ πατὴρ αὐτὴν ἐγγυήσῃ, 'if her father does not betroth her' (6.57.4). Yet a different impression is given by the account of an earlier incident in the life of Leotykhidas.

Hdt. 6.65.2. ὁ δὲ Λευτυχίδης ἦν ἐχθρὸς τῷ Δημαρήτῳ μάλιστα γεγονὼς διὰ πρῆγμα τοιόνδε· ἁρμοσαμένου Λευτυχίδεω Πέρκαλον τὴν Χίλωνος τοῦ Δημαρμένου θυγατέρα ὁ Δημάρητος ἐπιβουλεύσας ἀποστερέει Λευτυχίδεα τοῦ γάμου φθάσας αὐτὸς τὴν Πέρκαλον ἁρπάσας καὶ σχὼν γυναῖκα. 'Leotykhidas had become a bitter enemy of Demaratos because of the following incident. After Leotykhidas had engaged to himself Perkalos, the daughter of Khilon son of Demarmenos, Demaratos deprived Leotykhidas of the marriage by a plot: he got in first himself, seized Perkalos, and had her as his wife.'

One might be tempted to dismiss this as merely vivid language for saying that Demaratos (who was a king) browbeat Khilon into breaking off the betrothal of his daughter to Leotykhidas and betrothing her to Demaratos instead, but for the fact that Plutarch, in his account of Spartan marriage, also uses the verb ἁρπάζω, 'seize', and seems to mean it literally.

Plu. *Lyk.* 15.4-9. ἐγάμουν δὲ δι' ἁρπαγῆς, οὐ μικρὰς οὐδ' ἀώρους πρὸς γάμον, ἀλλ' [καὶ] ἀκμαζούσας καὶ πεπείρους. τὴν δ' ἁρπασθεῖσαν ἡ νυμφεύτρια καλουμένη παραλαβοῦσα, τὴν μὲν κεφαλὴν ἐν χρῷ περιέκειρεν, ἱματίῳ δ' ἀνδρείῳ καὶ ὑποδήμασιν ἐνσκευάσασα, κατέκλινεν ἐπὶ στιβάδα μόνην ἄνευ φωτός. ὁ δὲ νυμφίος οὐ μεθύων οὐδὲ θρυπτόμενος, ἀλλὰ νήφων ὥσπερ ἀεὶ δεδειπνηκὼς ἐν τοῖς φιδιτίοις, παρεισελθὼν ἔλυσε τὴν ζώνην καὶ μετήνεγκεν ἀράμενος ἐπὶ τὴν κλίνην. συνδιατρίψας δὲ χρόνον οὐ πολύν, ἀπῄει κοσμίως οὗπερ εἰώθει τὸ πρότερον καθευδήσων μετὰ τῶν ἄλλων νέων· καὶ τὸ λοιπὸν οὕτως ἔπραττε, τοῖς μὲν ἡλικιώταις συνδιημερεύων καὶ συναναπαυόμενος, πρὸς δὲ τὴν νύμφην κρύφα ⟨καὶ⟩ μετ' εὐλαβείας φοιτῶν, αἰσχυνόμενος καὶ δεδοικὼς μή τις αἴσθοιτο τῶν ἔνδον, ἅμα καὶ τῆς νύμφης ἐπιτεχνωμένης καὶ συνευπορούσης ὅπως ἂν ἐν καιρῷ καὶ λανθάνοντες ἀλλήλοις συμπορεύοιντο. καὶ τοῦτ' ἔπραττον οὐκ ὀλίγον χρόνον, ἀλλ' ὥστε καὶ παῖδας ἐνίοις γενέσθαι πρὶν ἐς ἡμέραν θεάσασθαι τὰς ἑαυτῶν γυναῖκας. 'They used to marry by seizure — not little girls or ones unripe for marriage, but in their prime and mature. When a woman was seized, the so-called bridesmaid received her, and she shaved her head, dressed her in a man's cloak and shoes, and laid her on a pallet alone without a light. The bridegroom, not intoxicated or enervated, but sober, after dining in his mess as usual, slipped in to her, loosed her girdle, and lifted her and carried her to the bed. After spending a short time with her, he went away in an orderly manner to sleep in his usual quarters, with the other young men; and so he went on, passing his days and his rest with men of his own age, and visiting his bride secretly and cautiously, being ashamed and afraid that someone in the house might see him. The bride too helped to contrive opportunities for them to come together unobserved. They went on like this for a considerable time, so that some men even had children before they saw their own wives in daylight.'

Plutarch is here describing the marriage of a man who has not yet reached the age of thirty, and so is still living in military quarters, not in his own house. He goes at night to the house of the woman he wishes to marry, and carries her off to the house of his own family. The 'so-called bridesmaid' is presumably a woman of the bridegroom's family, with whom the bride resides from then on. In this account the seizure is the taking of the bride from her old home to her new one. But a rather different kind of seizure is recounted in a fragment of Hermippos of Smyrna, who lived in the third century B.C.

> Ath. 555b-c. καὶ γὰρ τὰς γαμετὰς ὁ καλὸς ἡμῶν ἑστιάτωρ ἐπαινῶν Ἕρμιππον ἔφη ἐν τοῖς Περὶ νομοθετῶν ἱστορεῖν ὅτι ἐν Λακεδαίμονι εἰς οἴκημά τι σκοτεινὸν

πᾶσαι ἐνεκλείοντο αἱ κόραι, συνεγκλειομένων καὶ τῶν ἀγάμων νεανίσκων· καὶ ἕκαστος ἧς ἐπιλάβοιτο, ταύτην ἀπῆγεν ἄπροικον. διὸ καὶ Λύσανδρον ἐζημίωσαν, ὅτι καταλιπὼν τὴν προτέραν ἑτέραν ἐβουλεύετο περικαλλεστέραν ἀγαγέσθαι. 'For, when praising married women too, our fine host said that Hermippos records in his *On Legislators* that in Lakedaimon all the girls used to be shut up in a dark room, and all the unmarried young men were shut in with them; and each man took whichever girl he caught, without a dowry. This was why Lysander was punished, because he abandoned the first girl and tried to contrive to marry a prettier one.'

In studying Sparta it is not safe to dismiss a particular social arrangement as impossible merely on the ground that it seems preposterous to us. I am prepared to believe that the blind-man's-buff device was used on some occasions as a device for getting the young Spartans married. But it cannot have been the invariable method of making marriages; the passages from Herodotos show that many marriages, perhaps nearly all, were arranged individually. But even in those cases there seem to be alternative methods: betrothal (ἐγγύη, for which ἁρμόζειν may be regarded as a synonym), by which the father gives his daughter to a husband; and seizure (ἁρπαγή), by which the husband simply takes her. Perhaps the two are less incompatible than they seem. In our own churches it is customary for a bride to be 'given away' by her father, and yet at the same time a legal marriage can be made without the father's consent. So too in Sparta it will have been customary for a marriage to be arranged between the woman's father and the prospective husband; in such a case they probably agreed that the bridegroom would take the bride from her father's house on a certain night, and the

WOMEN AND MARRIAGE

'seizure' was a conventional formality. Yet it was also possible for a seizure to occur without the father's consent, and the result was a valid marriage, as the case of Demaratos shows. The conclusion must be that in Sparta, unlike Athens, formal betrothal by the bride's father was not required for a legal marriage.

When there was no formal betrothal, there cannot have been a formal undertaking by the father to give a dowry for his daughter. That presumption seems to be confirmed by one of the apophthegms attributed to Lykourgos, which testifies that he forbade dowries by law (and note ἄπροικον in the passage just quoted from Athenaios); and yet Aristotle says that large dowries were given.

Plu. *Eth.* 227f. πυνθανομένου δέ τινος διὰ τί τὰς κόρας ἐνομοθέτησεν ἀπροίκους ἐκδίδοσθαι, "ὅπως" ἔφη "μήτε δι᾽ ἔνδειαν ἄγαμοί τινες ἐαθῶσι μήτε διὰ περιουσίαν σπουδάζωνται, ἕκαστος δ᾽ εἰς τὸν τρόπον τῆς παιδὸς ἀφορῶν ἀρετῇ τὴν αἵρεσιν ποιῶνται". 'When someone asked why he legislated that girls should be given in marriage without dowries, he said "So that none may be either left unmarried because of poverty or sought eagerly because of affluence, but each man may concentrate his attention on the girl's character and make his choice on her merits".'

Arist. *Pol.* 1270a 23-5. ἔστι δὲ καὶ τῶν γυναικῶν σχεδὸν τῆς πάσης χώρας τῶν πέντε μερῶν τὰ δύο, τῶν τ᾽ ἐπικλήρων πολλῶν γινομένων, καὶ διὰ τὸ προῖκας διδόναι μεγάλας. 'And almost two-fifths of the land belongs to women, because there are many heiresses, and because large dowries are given.'

One way of dealing with this apparent conflict of evidence is to dismiss Plutarch's anecdote as a moralizing invention, someone's idea of what the ideal legislator ought to have said. But perhaps a better way is to explain it as a divergence between law and practice: it is credible that, although the law forbade a formal contract of marriage including an undertaking to give a dowry, in practice a father would often give a large gift to his daughter as soon as she was married.

There is little evidence about prohibited degrees of relationship for marriage in Sparta. That probably means that in this respect Sparta did not differ from the rest of Greece; if Spartans had married their own mothers or daughters, that would surely have provoked a comment from Herodotos or Plutarch. Herodotos does mention two instances of a man marrying his niece (5.39.1, 7.239.4), but that was acceptable in Athens too (e.g. Lys. 32.4, Dem. 44.10). The only point in doubt is marriage between a half-brother and a half-sister. In Athens marriage was permitted between siblings with the same father, provided that they had different mothers (Dem. 57.20, Plu. *Them.* 32.2), but Philo declares that the Spartan law was just the opposite, permitting marriage between siblings only if they had different fathers (*Special Laws* 3.22). No other evidence either contradicts or confirms Philo.

POLYGAMY

Another rule which generally goes without saying is monogamy. A man wishing to marry another wife had to divorce the previous one. He did this simply by sending her away ($\mathit{\dot{\alpha}\pi o\pi\acute{\epsilon}\mu\pi\epsilon\iota\nu}$, e.g. Hdt. 6.63.1), presumably back to her father's house. There is no evidence for any formal procedure or restriction to prevent a husband from doing this whenever he pleased, but what he could not do was to keep two wives simultaneously. This law is proved by an exception. King Anaxandridas had no children by his first wife, and the ephors urged him to divorce her and marry another, because

WOMEN AND MARRIAGE

the Spartans expected him to continue the royal line; but he rejected this advice, on the ground that his wife had done nothing to deserve such treatment. Herodotos recounts the sequel.

> Hdt. 5.40. πρὸς ταῦτα οἱ ἔφοροι καὶ οἱ γέροντες βουλευσάμενοι προσέφερον Ἀναξανδρίδῃ τάδε. "ἐπεὶ τοίνυν περιεχόμενόν σε ὁρῶμεν τῆς ἔχεις γυναικός, σὺ δὲ ταῦτα ποίεε καὶ μὴ ἀντίβαινε τούτοισι, ἵνα μή τι ἀλλοῖον περὶ σεῦ Σπαρτιῆται βουλεύσωνται. γυναικὸς μὲν τῆς ἔχεις οὐ προσδεόμεθά σευ τῆς ἐξέσιος, σὺ δὲ ταύτῃ τε πάντα ὅσα νῦν παρέχεις πάρεχε καὶ ἄλλην πρὸς ταύτῃ ἐσάγαγε γυναῖκα τεκνοποιόν." ταῦτά κῃ λεγόντων συνεχώρησε ὁ Ἀναξανδρίδης, μετὰ δὲ γυναῖκας ἔχων δύο διξὰς ἱστίας οἴκεε, ποιέων οὐδαμῶς Σπαρτιητικά.
> 'Therefore the ephors and the senators, after deliberation, made the following proposal to Anaxandridas. "Since we see that you are attached to your present wife, do as follows, and do not go against this, or the Spartiates may make some untoward decision about you. We do not request the dismissal of your present wife, but, while providing for her all that you provide at present, bring in another wife in addition to her to bear children." Such were their words, and Anaxandridas agreed; and afterwards he had two wives and inhabited two homes, a very unSpartan practice.'

In this case the ephors and the senate authorized an infringement of Spartan law. But in fact the law of monogamy was less simple at Sparta than elsewhere, since it was permitted for a woman to have sexual relations with two men.

> Xen. LP 1.7-9. εἴ γε μέντοι συμβαίη γεραιῷ νέαν ἔχειν, ὁρῶν τοὺς τηλικούτους φυλάττοντας μάλιστα τὰς

γυναῖκας, τἀναντία καὶ τούτου ἐνόμισε· τῷ γὰρ πρεσβύτῃ ἐποίησεν, ὁποίου ἀνδρὸς σῶμά τε καὶ ψυχὴν ἀγασθείη, τοῦτον ἐπαγαγομένῳ τεκνοποιήσασθαι. εἰ δέ τις αὖ γυναικὶ μὲν συνοικεῖν μὴ βούλοιτο, τέκνων δὲ ἀξιολόγων ἐπιθυμοίη, καὶ τοῦτο νόμιμον ἐποίησεν, ἥντινα [ἂν] εὔτεκνον καὶ γενναίαν ὁρῴη, πείσαντα τὸν ἔχοντα ἐκ ταύτης τεκνοποιεῖσθαι. καὶ πολλὰ μὲν τοιαῦτα συνεχώρει. αἵ τε ˙γὰρ γυναῖκες διττοὺς οἴκους βούλονται κατέχειν, οἵ τε ἄνδρες ἀδελφοὺς τοῖς παισὶ προσλαμβάνειν, οἳ τοῦ μὲν γένους καὶ τῆς δυνάμεως κοινωνοῦσι, τῶν δὲ χρημάτων οὐκ ἀντιποιοῦνται. 'If an old man had a young wife, seeing that men of that age guard their wives very closely, he (Lykourgos) thought up the opposite arrangement: he arranged for the elderly man to get children by bringing in any man whose physique and character he admired. And if a man did not wish to live with a wife but wanted to have fine children, he also made it legal for him, when he saw a woman of quality who had borne good children, to produce children by her with her husband's consent. And he permitted many such arrangements; the wives wish to control two households, and the husbands wish to get for their sons brothers who contribute to the strength of the family but do not claim a share of the property.'

Plu. *Lyk.* 15.12-13. ἐξῆν μὲν γὰρ ἀνδρὶ πρεσβυτέρῳ νέας γυναικός, εἰ δή τινα τῶν καλῶν καὶ ἀγαθῶν ἀσπάσαιτο νέων καὶ δοκιμάσειεν, εἰσαγαγεῖν παρ' αὐτὴν καὶ πλήσαντα γενναίου σπέρματος ἴδιον αὑτοῦ ποιήσασθαι τὸ γεννηθέν. ἐξῆν δὲ πάλιν ἀνδρὶ χρηστῷ, τῶν εὐτέκνων τινὰ καὶ σωφρόνων θαυμάσαντι γυναικῶν ἑτέρῳ γεγαμημένην, πείσαντι τὸν ἄνδρα συνελθεῖν, ὥσπερ ἐν χώρᾳ καλλικάρπῳ φυτεύοντα καὶ ποιούμενον παῖδας ἀγαθούς, ἀγαθῶν ὁμαίμους καὶ συγγενεῖς ἐσομένους. 'It was permitted for an elderly husband of a young wife, if he liked and approved of some fine young gentleman, to bring him in to her, and filling her with good seed, to adopt the offspring as his own. It was also permitted for a respectable man, if he admired another man's wife who had borne good children and was well behaved, to have intercourse with her with her husband's consent, sowing in a fertile field, so to speak, and producing good children, who would be blood-relatives of a good family.'

Polyb. 12.6b.8. παρὰ μὲν γὰρ τοῖς Λακεδαιμονίοις καὶ πάτριον ἦν καὶ σύνηθες τρεῖς ἄνδρας ἔχειν τὴν γυναῖκα καὶ τέτταρας, τοτὲ δὲ καὶ πλείους ἀδελφοὺς ὄντας, καὶ τὰ τέκνα τούτων εἶναι κοινά, καὶ γεννήσαντα παῖδας ἱκανοὺς ἐκδόσθαι γυναῖκά τινι τῶν φίλων καλὸν καὶ σύνηθες. 'For among the Lakedaimonians it was a traditional custom for three or four men to have the wife, sometimes more if they were brothers. The children of these belonged to them in common. When a man had begotten enough children, it was an honourable custom for him to give a wife away to one of his friends.'

The purpose of this law was evidently to maximize the Spartiate population by getting the women to produce as many strong children as possible. In all cases the consent of the woman's husband was necessary; and the law merely permitted such arrangements, not required them. (In Xen. *LP* 1.7 the word ἐποίησεν is wrongly translated 'requiring' by Marchant in the Loeb edition. Plutarch's ἐξῆν shows that the sense of permission is correct; cf. ἐποίησε in Xen. *LP* 6.3, and Ollier's note on 1.7 in his edition.) But a man who had a healthy young wife and was not producing children by her would probably come under strong moral pressure to allow another man to do so. Xenophon and Plutarch both make clear that the children born of such unions could be regarded legally as belonging either to their natural father or to their mother's husband; this was a matter for mutual agreement between the two men, made probably at the time of the original arrangement. Thus it was not important if there was uncertainty which of them was actually the father of a particular child. But the statement of Polybios that the children belonged to the two (or more) men in common should be rejected, because the phrases of both Xenophon (especially τῶν δὲ χρημάτων οὐκ ἀντιποιοῦνται) and Plutarch (especially ἴδιον αὑτοῦ ποιήσασθαι τὸ γεννηθέν) imply that each child belonged legally to only one of the men involved. On this point Polybios may have confused Sparta with some other state, possibly Plato's (cf. Pl. *Rep.* 457d), or he may have misinterpreted the remark attributed to Lykourgos that children were not their fathers' private property but κοινοὺς τῆς πόλεως (Plu. *Lyk.* 15.14).

Why then did Anaxandridas not take advantage of this law, begetting children by another man's wife while still keeping his own wife? Evidently because the birth of a royal heir was a special case. It was considered essential that a king should be a true son of the royal line; that is shown by the fates of Demaratos, who was deposed because he was believed not to be the son of the previous king (Hdt. 6.61-7), and of a later Leotykhidas, who was prevented from assuming the kingship for the same reason (Xen. *Hell.* 3.3.1-4). If Anaxandridas had had intercourse with another man's wife, the true paternity of any child she bore would have been questionable. Therefore it was essential that he should take a woman as his own wife and keep her in his own house, where no other man could associate with her. But the law did not allow him to do that as well as keeping his previous wife, until he was given special exemption from it. There was no legal objection to a man's having intercourse with two women; what was illegal was keeping two wives for himself in his own house.

Thus it is not easy to pin down a concept of adultery in Sparta. Nevertheless there was such a concept, or rather a concept of μοιχεία, better translated as 'seduction' than 'adultery', since it covered wrongful intercourse with either an unmarried or a married woman. Plutarch, after the passage just quoted, goes on to say that, in contrast to the licentiousness concerning women said to have existed later, in early Sparta the very existence of μοιχεία was disbelieved; and he tells an anecdote implying that no penalty for it was laid down (Plu. *Lyk.* 15.16-18). Aristotle also probably refers to sexual licence when he says that women in Sparta live a life which is self-indulgent in every way (Arist. *Pol.* 1269b 22-3). The rule about μοιχεία, observed in the early period but not later, must have been that a man might not have sexual intercourse with another man's wife unless the husband gave permission, nor with an unmarried woman unless, being unmarried himself, he carried her off to keep her in his own house (which would constitute marriage).

The concept of legitimacy must likewise have tended to disappear when a husband permitted another man to have intercourse with his wife. Xen. *LP* 1.7-9 and Plu. *Lyk.* 15.12-13 (quoted on pages 83-5) use the verbs ποιεῖσθαι and τεκνοποιεῖσθαι both of the husband and of the other man in such cases. The verb ποιεῖσθαι can mean either to acknowledge a child as one's own or to adopt a child begotten by someone else (compare, for example, Dem. 41.3 and 57.43), and the reason why it was not found inconvenient to use the same word for both acts is evidently that both had the same effect legally; if a man ποιεῖται a child, he is thenceforth the child's legal father, whatever the fact of paternity may have been.

V

Landholding and Inheritance

EQUAL LOTS OF LAND

It is stated in several texts that at an early date the land of Sparta was shared out equally among the citizens. The earliest surviving reference to this is in Plato. His account is brief and vague; he evidently assumes that the fact to which he is referring is well known. He says that legislators in the three Dorian states of Argos, Messene, and Sparta, when they made arrangements for equality of property (ἰσότητα τῆς οὐσίας), were able to divide up the land without disputes (γῆν ἀναμφισβητήτως διανέμεσθαι); however, two of the states later destroyed their constitution and laws, and only Sparta persisted with the arrangement (Pl. *Laws* 684d-685a). This appears to imply that equality of landholdings in Sparta still obtained in Plato's time. On this evidence alone it would be hard to say just what that meant, but we can supplement Plato's statement from Polybios and Plutarch.

Polybios refers to the matter in the course of a comparison between the Cretan and Spartan constitutions. He remarks that 'the ancient writers, Ephoros, Xenophon, Kallisthenes, and Plato' say that the two constitutions are similar, but are wrong to do so, because they record some significant differences between them; one of these is that in Sparta there is equal distribution of landholdings.

Polyb. 6.45.3. τῆς μὲν δὴ Λακεδαιμονίων πολιτείας ἴδιον εἶναί φασι πρῶτον μὲν τὰ περὶ τὰς ἐγγαίους κτήσεις, ὧν οὐδενὶ μέτεστι πλεῖον, ἀλλὰ πάντας τοὺς πολίτας ἴσον ἔχειν δεῖ τῆς πολιτικῆς χώρας. 'Peculiar to the Lakedaimonian constitution, they say, is, first, the arrangement concerning landholdings, of which no one man has a larger share, but all the citizens must hold an equal part of the land belonging to the city.'

'They say' must refer to the 'ancient writers' previously named. We have already seen that there is an allusion in Plato to equality of landholdings in Sparta, but no such allusion survives in Xenophon. It is unlikely that Polybios would have used the plural φασι if he had not found a reference to the matter in at least two of the four authors named; so probably the work, now lost, of either Ephoros or Kallisthenes or both gave some account of it. Indeed Ephoros may well be one of the sources of Plutarch's more detailed account.

> Plu. *Lyk.* 8.1, 5-7. δεύτερον δὲ τῶν Λυκούργου πολιτευμάτων καὶ νεανικώτατον ὁ τῆς γῆς ἀναδασμός ἐστι. . . . ἔνειμε τὴν μὲν ἄλλην τοῖς περιοίκοις Λακωνικὴν τρισμυρίους κλήρους, τὴν δ' εἰς τὸ ἄστυ τὴν Σπάρτην συντελοῦσαν ἐνακισχιλίους· τοσοῦτοι γὰρ ἐγένοντο κλῆροι Σπαρτιατῶν. ἔνιοι δέ φασι τὸν μὲν Λυκοῦργον ἑξακισχιλίους νεῖμαι, τρισχιλίους δὲ μετὰ ταῦτα προσθεῖναι Πολύδωρον· οἱ δὲ τοὺς μὲν ἡμίσεις τῶν ἐνακισχιλίων τοῦτον, τοὺς δ' ἡμίσεις Λυκοῦργον. ὁ δὲ κλῆρος ἦν ἑκάστου τοσοῦτος, ὥστ' ἀποφορὰν φέρειν ἀνδρὶ μὲν ἑβδομήκοντα κριθῶν μεδίμνους, γυναικὶ δὲ δώδεκα, καὶ τῶν ὑγρῶν καρπῶν ἀναλόγως τὸ πλῆθος. 'The second and boldest of Lykourgos's constitutional acts is his redistribution of the land. . . . He allocated the rest of Lakonia to the perioikoi in 30,000 lots, and the land belonging to the town of Sparta in 9,000; that was the number of

LANDHOLDING AND INHERITANCE

Spartiates' lots. But some say that Lykourgos allocated 6,000 and Polydoros added 3,000 later; and others that the latter allocated half of the 9,000 and Lykourgos half. Each man's lot was large enough to produce 70 medimnoi of barley for a man and 12 for a woman, with a proportionate amount of liquid products.'

It is clear that Plutarch had several sources of information available to him, and they agreed that the total number of lots (κλῆροι) in Lakonia was 9,000 for Spartiates and 30,000 for perioikoi, though there was disagreement about the stages by which the allocations were made. It is also clear that the land allocated to the Spartiates was the part of Lakonia regarded as pertaining to the city of Sparta (obviously the land nearest to it, probably the same area which Agis IV later proposed to reallot to Spartiates, 'from the watercourse down Pellene to Taygetos and Malea and Sellasia', Plu. *Agis* 8.1; that definition is not very clear, and 'Malea' may be mistaken or corrupt, but Forrest *Sparta* 135-6 is hardly justified in complaining 'No one tells us where in Laconia or Messenia the public land was to be found'), whereas the land allocated to the perioikoi pertained to the other towns and villages in Lakonia. Plutarch's τὴν εἰς τὸ ἄστυ τὴν Σπάρτην συντελοῦσαν was what Polybios calls τῆς πολιτικῆς χώρας. Some scholars (e.g. Walbank *Comm. on Polyb.* 1.729, Cartledge *Sparta* 166) pose the question whether πολιτική means 'owned by the city' or 'owned by the citizens', but Plutarch's phrase shows that it does not, in itself, mean either; it means only that the land belonged to the city in a political or administrative sense (as in English one may say 'The Isle of Arran belongs to Strathclyde'; cf. LSJ συντελέω III). As for the equality of the lots, Plutarch explains that this was measured by the amount which they would produce, rather than by the area which they covered, so that a lot of poor agricultural land would be larger in area than one of rich land. Polybios's word ἴσον does not have to mean 'equal in area', and should not be taken (as it is by Cartledge *Sparta* 166-7) as inconsistent with Plutarch's account. (On the lots given to the perioikoi, which may not have been equal to the Spartiates' or to one another, see page 28.)

Some modern scholars reject entirely the tradition that the Spartiates held equal lots of land. One suggestion, which was made by Grote and is accepted by Jones *Sparta* 43 (cf. Tigerstedt *Legend* 1.499 n.941), is that it is a myth invented in the late fourth or the third century to support the proposals for redistribution of land which were made at that period. But that suggestion can be dismissed at once, because we have already seen that it goes back at least as early as the time of Plato. Another objection made to the tradition of equal lots is that Plutarch's evidence is not consistent with the evidence of Arist. *Pol.* 1270a 15-34. However, that objection is unsound, because the passage of Aristotle refers to a later period, after the rhetra of Epitadeus changed the rules about property; the change will be considered later in this chapter.

A different kind of objection is that the Spartiates cannot have had equal lots of land because some of them are known to have been richer than others. One passage which has been said (by Walbank *Comm. on Polyb.* 1.730) to show that extremes of wealth and poverty had become apparent as early as the Second Messenian War does not really do so: this is Arist. *Pol.* 1306b 36-1307a 2, which refers to Tyrtaios's poem *Eunomia* as evidence of distress and of demands for a redistribution of land; but it is clear, both from Aristotle's phrase θλιβόμενοι γάρ τινες διὰ τὸν πόλεμον, 'for some men, in distress because of the war...', and from another account in Paus. 4.18.1-3, that the reason for the distress at that time

LANDHOLDING AND INHERITANCE

was only that temporarily some areas of Lakonia could not be farmed because of the Messenians' incursions, not that there was any lasting inequality in property or in prosperity. (Cozzoli *Proprietà* 34-5 wrongly interprets this evidence as referring to land in Messenia only; in fact Pausanias explicitly mentions the part of Lakonia which bordered on Messenia.) Nevertheless there is no doubt that by the fifth century some Spartiates were noticeably better off than others (Hdt. 7.134.2). How did that occur, if each had the same amount of land? One obvious answer is that, even at a time when there was no coinage and little precious metal, one man could become prosperous by organizing his farm efficiently, or by getting his slaves to manufacture useful articles, or by securing booty in war, while another could become poor when disease carried off his helots or his animals, or a fire burned down his house, or simply by thriftlessness. But an even better answer is that some Spartiates acquired additional land which was not part of the equal lots. For there is evidence that they held land in two categories.

> Herakleides Lembos *Exc. Pol.* (ed. Dilts) 12. πωλεῖν δὲ γῆν Λακεδαιμονίοις αἰσχρὸν νενόμισται. τῆς ἀρχαίας μοίρας οὐδὲ ἔξεστι. 'To sell land is considered shameful by the Lakedaimonians. To sell any of the ancient portion is not even allowed.'

> Plu. *Eth.* 238e. [...] τῆς ἀρχῆθεν διατεταγμένης μοίρας· πωλεῖν δ' οὐκ ἐξῆν. '... of the portion originally distributed; to sell it was not allowed.'

'The ancient portion' must surely refer to the equal lots; so these passages imply that some Spartiates held other land too. Since the equal allotments to Spartiates and perioikoi are said to have taken up the whole of Lakonia (Plu. *Lyk.* 8.5), the additional land was no doubt in territory of which they gained control later, primarily Messenia. How the land in Messenia was originally distributed we do not know. It could have been by another round of equal allotment, but, if so, the equality in this case will not have lasted, because, unlike the lots in Lakonia, these lots could be sold.

Yet another difficulty about the tradition that Spartiates held equal lots of land arises when we ask how the lots were passed on from one generation to the next. Plu. *Lyk.* 16.1 (quoted on pages 52-3) says that a newborn baby was inspected by the eldest members of the tribe, and if it was strong they ordered the father to rear it, 'allocating to it one of the 9,000 lots'. If this is interpreted strictly, it means that the elders had a number of unoccupied lots at their disposal, ready for allocation to babies; from which it necessarily follows that, to replenish the supply available for babies, each Spartiate's lot must have reverted to the tribe on his death. But that interpretation is contradicted by other evidence that lots were passed on from father to son, notably another passage of Plutarch himself, *Agis* 5.2 (quoted on pages 100-101), where he says that 'the families retained from one generation to another the number fixed by Lykourgos, and father left his lot to son'. This passage is quite explicit about inheritance; so Plutarch cannot have meant to deny inheritance in *Lyk.* 16.1. It seems, then, that the only possible interpretation of κλῆρον αὐτῷ τῶν ἐνακισχιλίων προσνείμαντες in *Lyk.* 16.1 is that the elders of the tribe formally pronounced that the baby would be entitled to succeed to possession of one of the 9,000 lots, not that they gave him a lot then and there. In the normal course of events he would take over his father's lot when his father died.

But what if a father had more than one son? Some modern scholars believe that the sons had then to share their father's lot, so that each got a smaller amount of land and thus it ceased to be true that all the Spartiates held equal lots (Walbank *Comm. on Polyb.* 1.730, Cozzoli *Proprietà* 5). But the reference in Xen. *LP* 1.9 to sharing τῶν χρημάτων probably refers to other kinds of property; the sharing of land lots between sons, though it doubtless happened in the fourth century (Arist. *Pol.* 1270b 5-6), does not seem to be part of the Lykourgan system as described by Plutarch, who insists in both passages (*Lyk.* 16.1, *Agis* 5.2) that the number of lots and households remained unaltered at 9,000. It can never really have been possible to maintain this number with absolute precision, but we can take Plutarch to mean that efforts were made to maintain it approximately. If so, that suggests the existence of three laws:

(*a*) A law prohibiting one person from holding two lots.

(*b*) A law about adoption, enabling one man's second or subsequent son to be adopted as heir by another man who had no son. The occasional mothax who became a citizen (see page 50) would also be a candidate for adoption (cf. Kahrstedt *Staatsrecht* 1.42).

(*c*) A law about daughters, enabling the lot of a man without sons to be held, after his death, by his daughter and her husband.

Despite the lack of clear evidence, several considerations make the existence of such laws about adoption and daughters probable. One is that those matters are known to have been prominent in laws about inheritance in the two other Greek cities from which we have most legal evidence (Athens and Gortyn). Another is that Plato in making laws for his imaginary city, which is to have a fixed number of lots of land, uses adoption and the marriage of daughters as principal means for maintaining a steady number of families (Pl. *Laws* 923c-926d); the possibility that Plato was influenced here by the Spartan example has been suggested by Asheri *Historia* 12 (1963) 18. Then there is the testimony of Herodotos that both adoption and the marriage of heiresses were subject to royal supervision.

> Hdt. 6.57.4-5. δικάζειν δὲ μούνους τοὺς βασιλέας τοσάδε μοῦνα· πατρούχου τε παρθένου πέρι, ἐς τὸν ἱκνέεται ἔχειν, ἢν μή περ ὁ πατὴρ αὐτὴν ἐγγυήσῃ, καὶ ὁδῶν δημοσιέων πέρι. καὶ ἤν τις θετὸν παῖδα ποιέεσθαι ἐθέλῃ, βασιλέων ἐναντίον ποιέεσθαι. 'And (it is granted) that the kings alone judge the following matters alone: concerning an unmarried heiress, the question to what man she passes as wife, if her father does not betroth her; and concerning public roads. And if anyone wishes to adopt a child, he has to do so in the presence of the kings.'

(In this passage the form πατρούχου is emended by Roehl and some other editors to πατρωιούχου. That is probably right, since what the girl held was not her father but her father's property; the Cretan form used in the law code of Gortyn is correspondingly πατροιôκος. Whether πατρωιοῦχος was the word used in Sparta is less clear; Herodotos may have merely used a word familiar to himself in Ionic, just as Arist. *Pol.* 1270a 24 and 27, referring to heiresses in Sparta, uses ἐπίκληρος which is the normal word in Attic. Others, most recently Karabélias *Studi Biscardi* 2.472, have suggested that ἐπιπαματίς (Hesykhios ε 5042) or ἐπιπταματίς (schol. on Pl. *Laws* 630e, *Souda* ε 2384) was a Spartan word for an heiress, but evidence that it was used in Sparta is lacking. In short, it is not known what word the Spartans themselves used for an heiress.)

The heiress in this passage is undoubtedly a woman whose father dies leaving no son, so that she is left with his property.

It is well known that in Athenian law a woman left in this position could be claimed in marriage by her father's nearest surviving male relative, to ensure that her father's property remained in the family. The law code of Gortyn too, lays down rules for the marriage of an heiress to a relative. It is therefore generally assumed that in Sparta the function of the kings concerning an heiress was to decide who was the nearest relative, who was to take the heiress in marriage. In fact there is no direct evidence that heiresses in Sparta had to be married to relatives. What the word ἰκνέεται means is simply that there were some rules about the matter (cf. Karabélias *Studi Biscardi* 2.473 n.14): the kings' function was not to choose a husband for the heiress according to their own preference, still less according to her preference, but to assess the claimants according to known criteria and thus to work out which man was entitled by law to marry her. What the criteria were, no text tells us. It is quite plausible that proximity of relationship was one of them, but it may not have been the only one. If we accept Plutarch's evidence that efforts were made to keep the number of families stable, we may postulate another criterion: that an heiress holding her father's lot of land in Lakonia should not be married to a man who already held such a lot or was heir apparent to his father's lot. There may, for all we know, have been other criteria too; for example, the claimant may have had to be of a suitable age for marriage. We can suppose that the kings awarded the heiress to the nearest relative who satisfied all the other criteria, whatever they were.

Similar conditions may have applied in cases of adoption. A Spartiate who had no children would be encouraged to adopt a young Spartiate as his son, to inherit his lot of land. But he would have to satisfy the kings that the man or boy whom he proposed to adopt was not already the holder of a lot or the heir apparent to one. It is possible that the kings also had other powers, not mentioned by Herodotos, to interfere with family arrangements to try to ensure the maintenance of the same number of families, each with one lot of land. In earlier times foreigners were sometimes given citizenship to make up the number of Spartiates (Arist. *Pol.* 1270a 34-6), but by the fifth century this was no longer done (see pages 50-1 for exceptions).

These suggestions about the system of inheritance and adoption are speculative, and may be wrong in details. But what is clear is that equality of lots of land should not be dismissed as impossible. In one way or another it would have been possible to maintain for several generations the system attributed to Lykourgos by Plutarch, by which each Spartiate held one of a number of lots of land of equal agricultural value in Lakonia (to which any land held in Messenia was additional); and there is no good reason why we should not accept this as a fact of the archaic period, even if we do not know exactly the time and circumstances in which the arrangement was made.

And if we accept the equal division of land, there is no reason to reject Plutarch's figure of 9,000 for the number of lots. This figure is not contradicted by other evidence. (The statement in Arist. *Pol.* 1270a 29-30, that the country could support 1,500 cavalry and 30,000 hoplites, is just an estimate of the maximum population that the fertile Eurotas valley would be able to feed, not a record of its actual population.) Plutarch reports three different accounts of the stages by which this total was reached: (*a*) Lykourgos allocated all 9,000 lots, (*b*) Lykourgos allocated 6,000 and Polydoros 3,000, (*c*) Lykourgos allocated 4,500 and Polydoros 4,500. Some scholars (e.g. Cartledge *Sparta* 169-70) have considered the figure of 9,000 to be an invention of the third century

LANDHOLDING AND INHERITANCE

because it is exactly twice the number of 4,500 lots into which Agis IV proposed to redivide the land held by Spartiates (Plu. *Agis* 8); Agis is assumed to have wanted a Lykourgan precedent for his figure. But that explanation is not satisfactory. If Agis had wanted simply to invent a precedent for 4,500 lots, the figure which he would have invented is 4,500, not 9,000. So a better explanation is that his figure of 4,500 was a deliberate halving (because of the fall in the number of Spartiates) of a figure of 9,000 which already existed, in the sense that 9,000 was known to have been the number of lots in earlier times. 'Agis had to settle for a smaller citizenry than 9,000, and the Lycurgan canon was adjusted accordingly' (Africa *CSCA* 1 (1968) 9). Plutarch's account (*c*) can plausibly be regarded as the account invented by Agis and his supporters, attempting to claim that 4,500 was the original number; the possibility that (*b*) was likewise due to the propaganda of Kleomenes III has also been suggested (cf. Marasco *Prometheus* 4 (1978) 118-19). But the version which Plutarch himself evidently favours, and which may well come from Aristotle's *LP*, is (*a*), that the number had been 9,000 all along. Nor is there any other objection to 9,000 as the approximate number of Spartiate households in the archaic period. It accords well enough with the figure of about 8,000 Spartiate men in 480 (Hdt. 7.234.2), which 'is the earliest reliable figure we have' (Cartledge *Sparta* 169).

THE RHETRA OF EPITADEUS

But in the fifth century the number of Spartiates was falling, the practice of enfranchising non-Spartiates had almost ceased, and it must have become impossible to find separate Spartiate heirs for 9,000 lots. That may be one reason why the system was changed. Plutarch attributes the change to a man named Epitadeus. (The best modern study of it is the article by Asheri in *Athenaeum* 39 (1961) 45-68; see also Christien *RHD* 52 (1974) 197-221, David *Sparta* 66-73).

Plu. *Agis* 5. ἀρχὴν μὲν οὖν διαφθορᾶς καὶ τοῦ νοσεῖν ἔσχε τὰ πράγματα τῶν Λακεδαιμονίων σχεδὸν ἀφ' οὗ τὴν Ἀθηναίων καταλύσαντες ἡγεμονίαν χρυσίου τε καὶ ἀργυρίου κατέπλησαν ἑαυτούς. οὐ μὴν ἀλλὰ καὶ τῶν οἴκων ὃν ὁ Λυκοῦργος ὥρισε φυλαττόντων ἀριθμὸν ἐν ταῖς διαδοχαῖς, καὶ πατρὸς παιδὶ τὸν κλῆρον ἀπολείποντος, ἁμῶς γέ πως ἡ τάξις αὕτη καὶ ἰσότης διαμένουσα τὴν πόλιν ἐκ τῶν ἄλλων ἀνέφερεν ἁμαρτημάτων. ἐφορεύσας δέ τις ἀνὴρ δυνατός, αὐθάδης δὲ καὶ χαλεπὸς τὸν τρόπον, Ἐπιτάδευς ὄνομα, πρὸς τὸν υἱὸν αὐτῷ γενομένης διαφορᾶς, ῥήτραν ἔγραψεν ἐξεῖναι τὸν οἶκον αὐτοῦ καὶ τὸν κλῆρον ᾧ τις ἐθέλοι καὶ ζῶντα δοῦναι καὶ καταλιπεῖν διατιθέμενον. οὗτος μὲν οὖν αὐτοῦ τινα θυμὸν ἀποπιμπλὰς ἴδιον εἰσήνεγκε τὸν νόμον· οἱ δ' ἄλλοι πλεονεξίας ἕνεκα δεξάμενοι καὶ κυρώσαντες, ἀπώλεσαν τὴν ἀρίστην κατάστασιν. ἐκτῶντο γὰρ ἀφειδῶς ἤδη παρωθοῦντες οἱ δυνατοὶ τοὺς προσήκοντας ἐκ τῶν διαδοχῶν, καὶ ταχὺ τῆς εὐπορίας εἰς ὀλίγους συρρυείσης, πενία τὴν πόλιν κατέσχεν, ἀνελευθερίαν καὶ τῶν καλῶν ἀσχολίαν ἐπιφέρουσα μετὰ φθόνου καὶ δυσμενείας πρὸς τοὺς ἔχοντας. ἀπελείφθησαν οὖν ἑπτακοσίων οὐ πλείονες Σπαρτιᾶται, καὶ τούτων ἴσως ἑκατὸν ἦσαν οἱ γῆν κεκτημένοι καὶ κλῆρον· ὁ δ' ἄλλος ὄχλος ἄπορος καὶ ἄτιμος ἐν τῇ πόλει παρεκάθητο, τοὺς μὲν ἔξωθεν πολέμους ἀργῶς καὶ ἀπροθύμως ἀμυνόμενος, ἀεὶ δέ τινα καιρὸν ἐπιτηρῶν μεταβολῆς καὶ μεταστάσεως τῶν παρόντων. 'The corruption and sickness of the Lakedaimonians' affairs first began about the time when they put a stop to the Athenians' dominance and gorged themselves on gold and silver. Nevertheless, as long as the families retained from one generation to another the

number fixed by Lykourgos, and father left his lot to
son, somehow this arrangement and continuing equality rescued the city from its other errors. But when a
certain powerful man became an ephor, a man wilful
and difficult in character, named Epitadeus, who had
quarrelled with his son, he proposed a rhetra that it
should be permitted both to give one's own house and
lot to whoever one wished during one's lifetime and to
bequeath them by will. So this man introduced the law
to satisfy a personal annoyance; but the rest accepted
and passed it for the sake of gain, and so destroyed their
excellent constitution. For the successful men now
began acquiring property unsparingly, pushing the
relatives out of the succession; and soon prosperity was
concentrated in a few men and poverty prevailed in the
city, bringing with it a lack of freedom and a lack of
leisure for the life of honour, together with envy and
hostility towards the affluent. So no more than seven
hundred Spartiates were left, and of those perhaps one
hundred were the ones who possessed land and a lot.
The rest of the mob, without resources and without
rights, sat in the city, defending it sluggishly and
unenthusiastically against external enemies, and always
watching for an opportunity for change and
revolution.'

Plutarch here records a change in the law, to permit a
Spartiate to give his house and his lot of land in Lakonia to
anyone he wished, either during his life or at his death.
Aristotle, in a passage criticizing the Spartan constitution,
evidently refers to the period after this change was made.

Arist. *Pol.* 1270a 15-34. μετὰ γὰρ τὰ νῦν ῥηθέντα τοῖς
περὶ τὴν ἀνωμαλίαν τῆς κτήσεως ἐπιτιμήσειεν ἄν τις.

τοῖς μὲν γὰρ αὐτῶν συμβέβηκε κεκτῆσθαι πολλὴν λίαν οὐσίαν, τοῖς δὲ πάμπαν μικράν· διόπερ εἰς ὀλίγους ἧκεν ἡ χώρα. τοῦτο δὲ καὶ διὰ τῶν νόμων τέτακται φαύλως· ὠνεῖσθαι μὲν γάρ, ἢ πωλεῖν τὴν ὑπάρχουσαν, ἐποίησεν οὐ καλόν, ὀρθῶς ποιήσας, διδόναι δὲ καὶ καταλείπειν ἐξουσίαν ἔδωκε τοῖς βουλομένοις· καίτοι ταὐτὸ συμβαίνειν ἀναγκαῖον ἐκείνως τε καὶ οὕτως. ἔστι δὲ καὶ τῶν γυναικῶν σχεδὸν τῆς πάσης χώρας τῶν πέντε μερῶν τὰ δύο, τῶν τ' ἐπικλήρων πολλῶν γινομένων, καὶ διὰ τὸ προῖκας διδόναι μεγάλας. καίτοι βέλτιον ἦν μηδεμίαν ἢ ὀλίγην ἢ καὶ μετρίαν τετάχθαι. νῦν δ' ἔξεστι δοῦναί τε τὴν ἐπίκληρον ὅτῳ ἂν βούληται, κἂν ἀποθάνῃ μὴ διαθέμενος, ὃν ἂν καταλίπῃ κληρονόμον, οὗτος ᾧ ἂν θέλῃ δίδωσιν. τοιγαροῦν δυναμένης τῆς χώρας χιλίους ἱππεῖς τρέφειν καὶ πεντακοσίους, καὶ ὁπλίτας τρισμυρίους, οὐδὲ χίλιοι τὸ πλῆθος ἦσαν. γέγονε δὲ διὰ τῶν ἔργων αὐτῶν δῆλον ὅτι φαύλως αὐτοῖς εἶχε τὰ περὶ τὴν τάξιν ταύτην· μίαν γὰρ πληγὴν οὐχ ὑπήνεγκεν ἡ πόλις, ἀλλ' ἀπώλετο διὰ τὴν ὀλιγανθρωπίαν. 'After what has just been mentioned, one might criticize the matter of the inequality of ownership. Some of them are in the position of owning too much property, while others have very little indeed; consequently the land has come into the hands of a few. This is also badly arranged by law; for he (the legislator) quite rightly made it dishonourable to buy property or to sell what one has, but he permitted those who wished to give it away and to bequeath it, and yet the result is bound to be the same either way. Also, nearly two-fifths of the whole country belongs to the women, because there are many heiresses, and because of giving large dowries. It would have been better if no dowry or a small one or even a medium-sized one had been fixed. As it is, one can give the heiress to whoever one wishes;

LANDHOLDING AND INHERITANCE

and if one dies without making a will, whoever one leaves as heir gives her to whoever he wishes. Therefore, although the country can support 1,500 cavalry and 30,000 hoplites, the number was less than 1,000. The events themselves have shown that they had these matters badly arranged; for the city could not bear one defeat, but was ruined because of shortage of population.'

Aristotle's statement that it was permitted to give away or bequeath property links this passage to Plutarch's statement that the rhetra of Epitadeus made it legal to give away or to bequeath one's house and lot. It is clear that Aristotle, writing of his own time, refers to the state of law which according to Plutarch did not exist until Epitadeus introduced his rhetra.

However, some modern scholars have used this fact to argue against the existence of the rhetra of Epitadeus, on the ground that Aristotle does not say that the permitting of gifts and bequests was an innovation but attributes it to the original legislator, Lykourgos (Forrest *Sparta* 137, Cartledge *Sparta* 165-8). But this is a misinterpretation of Aristotle. Aristotle is criticizing the laws of Sparta as they stood in the fourth century, when the military downfall of Sparta occurred. He discusses the purposes and effects of the various laws, but in doing so he does not personify the law by using expressions like 'the law intends . . .' or 'the law allows . . .'; his manner is rather to attribute intentions or actions to ὁ νομοθέτης, 'the legislator'. This noun is not a synonym for Lykourgos, who is mentioned only in sentences governed by φασί, as a remote figure for whose activities Aristotle does not vouch (1270a 6-8, 1271b 24-30). It simply means 'the author of the law under discussion'. There is a good example in 1270b 1-4 (quoted on page 76) where Aristotle says 'Wishing that the Spartiates should be as many as possible, the legislator encourages the citizens to produce as many children as possible; for they have a law that a man who has begotten three sons is to be exempt from military service...'; this is not an attribution of the law in question to Lykourgo<. Likewise in the passage with which we are now concerned, the noun to be understood as the subject of the verbs ἐποίησεν and ἔδωκε is ὁ νομοθέτης (from 1269b 20, at the start of the discussion of women and property; the sentence mentioning Lykourgos, 1270a 6-8, is parenthetic), meaning whoever was responsible for the law mentioned here. This says absolutely nothing about the date or origin of the law. Thus there is nothing in Aristotle which contradicts Plutarch's statement that the law was one proposed by Epitadeus, making a change in the Lykourgan system.

To what date, then, are Epitadeus and his rhetra to be assigned? Plutarch seems to mean that the rhetra was introduced some considerable time after the defeat of Athens in 404. His sequence is (*a*) Sparta defeated Athens, (*b*) the Spartans acquired much gold and silver but still maintained the number of families fixed by Lykourgos, (*c*) the rhetra of Epitadeus was passed, (*d*) serious decline set in. But this produces a tight timetable; for Aristotle's reference to the 'one defeat' of Sparta at Leuktra means that the law about property had caused a decline in manpower by 371 (whether or not that was the reason for the defeat itself; cf. Cawkwell *CQ* 33 (1983) 385), but a fall in the number of Spartiates could only have been a long-term effect, occurring in the course of generations.

In fact it is certain that some decrease had already begun in the fifth century (cf. Christien *RHD* 52 (1974) 203-8). Perhaps the rhetra of Epitadeus was just a contributory

LANDHOLDING AND INHERITANCE

factor, accelerating the decline in population which had begun earlier; perhaps Aristotle just did not know the date of Epitadeus and wrongly assumed that the law permitting gifts and bequests was older than it actually was. But a better solution is to date the rhetra of Epitadeus earlier than 404. For Plutarch does not in fact give any clear date for it. His essential point is simply that its bad effects became obvious some time after 404. A possible explanation may be that his source (perhaps Ephoros) mentioned the rhetra of Epitadeus in connection with the decline of Sparta which led to the defeat at Leuktra, and Plutarch failed to realize that that must imply a considerably earlier date for the rhetra. But whether that explanation is right or not, it seems best, while not rejecting Plutarch's testimony that the rhetra was proposed by Epitadeus, to accept from Aristotle the implication that it was a generation or two before Leuktra. Consequently the suggestion that Epitadeus was identical with a Spartan commander named by Thucydides as Epitadas, who died at Sphakteria in 425 (Thuc. 4.8.9, etc.), ought not to be dismissed as 'quite out of the question' (Michell *Sparta* 216-217), though there is no strong reason to accept it.

Altogether it appears reasonable to believe that Epitadeus proposed his rhetra, and the Spartans accepted it, some time in the last third of the fifth century. What exactly did it permit? According to Plutarch it permitted a Spartiate to give his house and lot during his lifetime, or to bequeath them at his death, to anyone he wished. This (τὸν οἶκον αὐτοῦ καὶ τὸν κλῆρον) evidently refers to his real property within the territory of the city of Sparta (what Plu. *Lyk.* 8.5 calls τὴν εἰς τὸ ἄστυ τὴν Σπάρτην συντελοῦσαν); we can take it as implying that a gift or bequest of other property, including land in Messenia, which was not part of the 9,000 lots, was permitted before. Plutarch considers that the rhetra led directly to a decrease in the number of landholdings, and it is clear that its essential point must have been to remove the ban on holding more than one of the 9,000 lots, so that from now on some individuals became able to build up large estates by combining a number of the lots.

But there is an obscurity about sale. Plutarch does not say that Epitadeus permitted the lots to be sold. Aristotle says that the legislator made it dishonourable to buy or sell property; we should call that a convention rather than a law, but since νόμος covers both kinds of rule Aristotle would see no difficulty in attributing it to a νομοθέτης. Herakleides Lembos (quoted on page 93) repeats that sale of land is considered shameful by the Spartans, and adds that sale of 'the ancient portion' is not even allowed. The present tense used by Herakleides may refer to his own time (the second century) or, more probably, may be copied from Aristotle's lost *LP*, but in either case it should refer to the period after Epitadeus. It seems best to accept what Herakleides says, and to conclude that Epitadeus made no change in the existing law that real property in the territory of the city of Sparta could not be sold. Why then has Aristotle omitted that point? Probably because it does not affect his argument in *Pol.* 1270a 18-22. In this passage his concern is to stress how easily Spartans could dispose of their land, not to mention restrictions which prevented them from doing so. And, as he says, 'the result is bound to be the same either way'. Permitting gift is almost equivalent to permitting sale, because of the difficulty in distinguishing one from the other. Sale could easily be disguised as gift by saying, for example, 'If you pay my debts for me, I will give you this piece of land'.

An even more obscure subject is mortgage. Plutarch refers to the burning of records of debtors, called κλάρια, in the third century (*Agis* 13.3), and this has been taken as evidence of the mortgaging of property. But the word κλάριον probably just means 'token' (originally for casting lots, and thence perhaps a voucher for other purposes) and is not necessarily connected with κλᾶρος meaning 'land lot'; it is just some kind of IOU held by a moneylender. Nor does Plutarch's statement a few lines earlier that Agesilaos (the uncle of Agis IV) did not want to lose his land (*Agis* 13.2) necessarily mean that his land was mortgaged; it may mean simply that, having no money, he had no way to appease his creditors except by giving them land. There is no earlier evidence of mortgage in Sparta.

After his comments on the alienability of land, Aristotle goes on to give information about heiresses in the fourth century: 'one can give the heiress to whoever one wishes; and if one dies without making a will, whoever one leaves as heir gives her to whoever he wishes' (*Pol.* 1270a 26-9, quoted on pages 102-3). This must refer to a different arrangement from the fifth-century one mentioned in Hdt. 6.57.4 (quoted on page 96) by which an heiress passed to a husband in accordance with rules under the supervision of the kings. The best way of explaining the change is to link it with the rhetra of Epitadeus: it is another aspect of the relaxation of the rule that no one might hold more than one of the 9,000 lots, and may well have formed part of that rhetra. Thenceforth a father with no son could seek out the best husband for his daughter without restricting his choice to those Spartiates, generally younger sons, who had no lot.

The more difficult part of Aristotle's sentence is the clause referring to the heir of a man who died without making a will. Presumably the heir in this case was the nearest male relative, but the way in which the terms ἐπίκληρος and κληρονόμος are used here seems, on the face of it, paradoxical or even self-contradictory. If a woman was left with the lot or estate (which is what ἐπίκληρος means), how could a man other than her husband be the taker of the lot or estate (which is what κληρονόμος means)? Aristotle is probably using Athenian rather than Spartan terminology, but comparison with Athenian texts using these words does not help here: in Athenian law, where there is an ἐπίκληρος, there is no heir except her eventual son, and the only instance which I have found of a man who is called κληρονόμος in a case in which a woman is ἐπίκληρος (Men. *Aspis* 85) is a relative who expects to marry her himself and take control of the property in that way. If in Sparta too all the property stayed with the ἐπίκληρος and her husband, how could another man be called κληρονόμος? Evidently the property was divided in some way, so that the ἐπίκληρος and the κληρονόμος each kept part of it. In fact something similar to this could happen in Athens in certain cases: there, if a man adopted his stepson as his heir and also left a daughter, the adopted son could not follow the normal practice of marrying the daughter, because she was his own half-sister by the same mother, and so he gave her in marriage to another man and the property was divided between them, though it was inherited by the daughter's son eventually (Isaios 3.45-51, Men. *Dyskolos* 729-39, *Aspis* 279-281). In Sparta, it appears from Aristotle's account, the heir had to give her to a husband with part of the property (we do not know how much) but could keep the rest of the property permanently.

But perhaps by Aristotle's time it was more usual that a man with no son did make a will. He could bequeath his property to anyone he wished; thus he could bequeath it all to his daughter, and that may well have been the commonest course. That would explain Aristotle's statement that a large part of the country now belonged to women 'because there are many heiresses'. Agiatis is a third-century example of a woman who was the heiress of large property belonging to her father (Plu. *Kleom.* 1.2). Even if he did have a son, a man could still bequeath property to his daughter, or give it to her as a dowry when she was married. Furthermore, it seems that property which a woman received as an heiress, or by way of dowry, was at her own disposal (cf. Schaps *Economic Rights* 88). In Athens such property had to be retained by her husband and was passed on eventually to her sons; she could not dispose of it. But in Sparta, besides Aristotle's statement that much of the country belonged to women, in the next century Agis IV, as part of his efforts at reforming Sparta, asked rich women, including his own mother and grandmother, to give up their wealth (Plu. *Agis* 4.1, 7.1-7, 9.6); his mother indeed lent money to many people (Plu. *Agis* 6.7). The earliest known instance of a wealthy woman in Sparta seems to be Kyniska, sister of king Agesilaos, in the first half of the fourth century (Xen. *Ages.* 9.6). So probably the rights of women to own and to dispose of wealth were part of the reform introduced by Epitadeus.

The revolutionary character of these changes has correctly been emphasized by Asheri *Historia* 12 (1963) 12-13. The rights of relatives to inherit property, which were very strong in Athens and other Greek cities, as far as our knowledge goes, had long been weaker in Sparta, where priority had been given to maintaining equality in landholdings in Lakonia. When the rhetra of Epitadeus made it possible to ignore both equality and family, that gave Spartiates an unusual degree of freedom to dispose of their property as they wished. The reasons why the changes were made are obscure. Plutarch may be correct, for all we know, in saying that Epitadeus had a purely personal reason for making his proposal, but the Spartiates in general must have had some further reason for accepting it. Perhaps, as Christien *RHD* 52

(1974) 197-221 argues, some of them had got into debt and wanted to extricate themselves from their difficulties by giving or bequeathing property to their creditors. Perhaps the fall in the number of Spartiates was a factor; it must have become impossible to find 9,000 Spartiate owners for the lots, and it would naturally be thought a bad thing to leave many lots occupied only by helots. But whatever the motives for the change, the consequence, as Aristotle and Plutarch both emphasize, was a tendency for property to become concentrated in even fewer hands, because a man choosing an heir, or choosing a husband for his daughter, tended to prefer one who was already prosperous and could do him some favour in return. Conversely, younger brothers in a large family could no longer expect that each of them would get a chance to inherit the lot of some childless man; all they could do was to share their father's property, getting only a small amount each; and, as Arist. *Pol.* 1270b 5-6 says, 'when the country is divided in this way, many are bound to become poor'. If they had been Athenian, they could have made a living as manufacturers, traders, or sailors, and still have remained citizens. But such activities were not open to citizens in Sparta. A man who worked in any of those ways was not living 'the life of honour' and so forfeited his status as a peer; but if he did no work and also owned no land, he would probably be unable to keep up his contributions to a mess and would lose his status that way. Thus the number of Spartiates was diminished.

VI

The Austere Life

FOOD AND DRINK

One of the best known features of Spartan society was the mess. This was a kind of dining club, for which the regular Spartan word was φειδείτιον (*IG* 5(1) 128.13, 150.1, 155.6) or φειδίτιον (*IG* 5(1) 1507.1). Attic authors sometimes call it φιδίτιον (the shortness of the first syllable is all but guaranteed by the metre in Antiphanes 44.3); sometimes they translate it into Attic as συσσίτιον. (For comment on the formation of the word φιδίτιον see Plu. *Lyk.* 12.1-2.) Other words used for it are ἀνδρεῖον (Alkman 98 Page) and συσκήνιον (Xen. *LP* 5.2). The institution receives unfavourable comment from Aristotle, who makes clear that membership was a requirement for citizenship.

> Arist. *Pol.* 1271a 26-37. οὐ καλῶς δ' οὐδὲ περὶ τὰ συσσίτια τὰ καλούμενα φιδίτια νενομοθέτηται τῷ καταστήσαντι πρῶτον. ἔδει γὰρ ἀπὸ κοινοῦ μᾶλλον εἶναι τὴν σύνοδον, καθάπερ ἐν Κρήτῃ· παρὰ δὲ τοῖς Λάκωσιν ἕκαστον δεῖ φέρειν, καὶ σφόδρα πενήτων ἐνίων ὄντων καὶ τοῦτο τὸ ἀνάλωμα οὐ δυναμένων δαπανᾶν, ὥστε συμβαίνει τοὐναντίον τῷ νομοθέτῃ τῆς προαιρέσεως. βούλεται μὲν γὰρ δημοκρατικὸν εἶναι τὸ κατασκεύασμα τῶν συσσιτίων, γίνεται δ' ἥκιστα δημοκρατικὸν οὕτω νενομοθετημένον. μετέχειν μὲν γὰρ οὐ ῥᾴδιον τοῖς λίαν πένησιν, ὅρος δὲ τῆς πολιτείας οὗτός ἐστιν αὐτοῖς ὁ

πάτριος, τὸν μὴ δυνάμενον τοῦτο τὸ τέλος φέρειν μὴ μετέχειν αὐτῆς. 'Nor has the law about the messes, the so-called *phiditia*, been well framed by the man who first established them. The income ought rather to have come from a common fund, as in Crete; but among the Lakonians each individual has to contribute, even though some men are very poor and unable to bear this expense, so that the result is the reverse of the legislator's intention. He wishes the arrangement of the messes to be democratic, but it turns out quite undemocratic when framed in this way; for it is difficult for the very poor to be members, and yet it is a traditional definition of their citizenship that a man who cannot make this payment is not a citizen.'

The same point is made again more briefly in Arist. *Pol.* 1272a 13-15. The amounts of the contributions which each member of a mess had to make each month are said by Plutarch to have been 1 medimnos of barley-meal, 8 khoes of wine, 5 mnai of cheese, $2\frac{1}{2}$ mnai of figs, and 'a very small amount of money' for buying additional items of food (*Lyk.* 12.3). (A description of Spartan meals, including figures slightly different from Plutarch's but qualified by 'about' and 'approximately', is given by Ath. 141a-c, quoting Dikaiarkhos.) The figures may be incorrect (the amount of wine in particular seems too large; cf. Michell *Sparta* 288-90), and we are not in a position to judge how many Spartiates were too poor to make the contributions, but we must accept Aristotle's word for it that it was legally possible for a man to be excluded from citizenship for this reason. (Thus the statement in Xen. *LP* 10.7, quoted on page 43, that poverty was no bar to citizenship, is not strictly true. But probably Xenophon means only that Spartiates of quite modest

THE AUSTERE LIFE

resources could be citizens, by contrast with cities governed by an oligarchy of the rich; he is not thinking of the really destitute.)

A young man would join a mess as soon as he came of age. Thus in Plu. *Lyk*. 15.6-7 (quoted on pages 78-9) the bridegroom has dined in his mess, while being still one of the young men.

Plutarch tells us that a mess had about fifteen members (*Lyk*. 12.3), and describes the method of secret ballot which they used for electing a new member (*Lyk*. 12.9-11). One adverse vote (like a 'black ball' in an old-fashioned English club) was enough to exclude a candidate. This seems to mean that it was possible for a man to be excluded from citizenship simply because he was unpopular and could get no mess to elect him unanimously. Or could several such men club together to form a new mess, and qualify for citizenship in that way? There is no information for answering this question. Perhaps failure to be elected to any mess at all was unknown, so that the question never arose; indeed, as the number of Spartiates gradually diminished, the practical problem may have been rather that some messes had difficulty in getting enough members to avoid having to close down or amalgamate with one another. On the whole it seems likely that the purpose of requiring a Spartiate to be a member of a mess was not primarily to exclude anyone who was unpopular, but to ensure that every Spartiate would make the effort to live with others on equal terms, and not be a recluse or a snob.

No Spartiate was allowed to dine at home, except when he cooked an animal after a sacrifice or a hunt, and then he had to send part of the meat to the mess for his comrades (Plu. *Lyk*. 12.4). Nor could drinking-parties be held at home: Xenophon commends the institution of the mess on the ground that a man will not drink too much if he knows that he has to walk home afterwards (*LP* 5.7), and Plato makes a Spartan speaker boast that the law makes symposia and drunkenness unknown throughout Lakonia (*Laws* 637a).

PERSONAL PROPERTY

A few other laws are known which are relevant to the austerity of Spartan life. There was one about the construction of houses: no tool but an axe was permitted for making the roof, and no tool but a saw for making the doors (Plu. *Lyk.* 13.5). The purpose of this was to keep houses simple; and the difference between houses in Sparta and in wealthy Corinth is illustrated by Plutarch's anecdote that king Leotykhidas, on a visit to Corinth, gazed at the workmanship of the ceiling and asked his host if square trees grew there. But in the same passage (*Lyk.* 13.6-7) Plutarch comments that cheap houses discourage expensive furniture; this implies that expensive furniture was not actually forbidden by law.

Women were not allowed to have jewellery, and, unlike Spartiate men, they had to keep their hair short.

> Herakleides Lembos *Exc. Pol.* (ed. Dilts) 13. τῶν ἐν Λακεδαίμονι γυναικῶν κόσμος ἀφῄρηται, οὐδὲ κομᾶν ἔξεστιν, οὐδὲ χρυσοφορεῖν. 'Women in Lakedaimon are deprived of adornment, and they are not allowed to grow long hair, nor to wear gold.'

Apart from his land, his house, and his armour, a Spartan's most valuable possessions would normally have been his slaves, horses, and dogs. It was a point of remark that the Spartans were exceptionally free in lending and borrowing these things among themselves (Xen. *LP* 6.3, Arist. *Pol.* 1263a 35-7), but that should be regarded as a matter of custom rather than law.

TRAVEL

It was another notorious feature of Sparta that communication with foreigners was discouraged. Spartiates were not allowed to go abroad except on public business, nor foreigners to settle in Sparta; and Aristotle and Plutarch are probably right to say that the main reason for this was to prevent the austerity of Spartan life from being corrupted by foreign influences (Arist. fr. 543, Plu. *Lyk.* 27.6-7, *Eth.* 238d). But it is significant that Xenophon, in a chapter added late to *LP* (see pages 8-14), regards this segregation as a thing of the past.

> Xen. *LP* 14.4. ἐπίσταμαι δὲ καὶ πρόσθεν τούτου ἕνεκα ξενηλασίας γιγνομένας καὶ ἀποδημεῖν οὐκ ἐξόν, ὅπως μὴ ῥᾳδιουργίας οἱ πολῖται ἀπὸ τῶν ξένων ἐμπίμπλαιντο. 'And I know that in former times it was for this reason that expulsions of aliens used to occur and travel abroad was not permitted, so that the citizens might not be infected with slackness from the foreigners.'

Occasions when aliens were expelled from Sparta are mentioned in the fifth century (Thuc. 1.144.2, 2.39.1, Ar. *Birds* 1012-13, and the dramatic date of Pl. *Prot.* 342c is in the fifth century), but not later. These must have been particular instances of administrative action, probably by the ephors, not necessarily on the basis of any permanent law. But the ban on Spartans' going abroad must have been a permanent law; that is implied by the use of οὐκ ἐξεῖναι in this connection in Xen. *LP* 14.4, Arist. fr. 543, Plu. *Eth.* 238d. Or perhaps there were two laws; that is suggested by comparison of the following passages of Plutarch.

> Plu. *Lyk.* 27.6. ὅθεν οὐδ' ἀποδημεῖν ἔδωκε τοῖς βουλομένοις καὶ πλανᾶσθαι, ξενικὰ συνάγοντας ἤθη καὶ

μιμήματα βίων ἀπαιδεύτων καὶ πολιτευμάτων διαφόρων. 'Hence he (Lykourgos) also did not permit those who wished to go abroad and travel around, gathering foreign habits and imitating uneducated ways of life and different political activities.'

Plu. *Agis* 11.2. ... κατὰ δή τινα νόμον παλαιόν, ὃς οὐκ ἐᾷ τὸν Ἡρακλείδην ἐκ γυναικὸς ἀλλοδαπῆς τεκνοῦσθαι, τὸν δ' ἀπελθόντα τῆς Σπάρτης ἐπὶ μετοικισμῷ πρὸς ἑτέρους ἀποθνῄσκειν κελεύει. '... in accordance with a certain old law, which forbids any of the Herakleidai to beget children by a foreign woman, and orders that any man who has left Sparta to settle among other people should die.'

The difference between πλανᾶσθαι and ἐπὶ μετοικισμῷ should be noticed. The law mentioned in *Agis* 11.2 is about a man who leaves Sparta in order to live permanently somewhere else (perhaps to avoid military service in wartime; compare the similar Athenian law mentioned in Hyp. *Ath*. 29), and then wants to return to Sparta when circumstances have changed; he is to be put to death if he reappears in Sparta. But the law mentioned in *Lyk*. 27.6 is about a man who just makes visits to other cities (without being sent there as a soldier or ambassador) and then comes home again; his penalty would probably be less severe than death. But both laws ceased to be enforced, as is clear from πρόσθεν (Xen. *LP* 14.4) and παλαιόν (Plu. *Agis*. 11.2).

MONEY

It was an essential part of the Lykourgan system that the Spartiates did not devote their time to money-making activities, but to soldiering. Agricultural work and manufacturing were done by the helots and perioikoi, and Spartiates were forbidden to engage in them.

Xen. *LP* 7.2. ἐν δὲ τῇ Σπάρτῃ ὁ Λυκοῦργος τοῖς ἐλευθέροις τῶν μὲν ἀμφὶ χρηματισμὸν ἀπεῖπε μηδενὸς ἅπτεσθαι. 'In Sparta Lykourgos forbade the free men to engage in anything concerned with money-making.'

Plu. *Lyk.* 24.2. τέχνης μὲν ἅψασθαι βαναύσου τὸ παράπαν οὐκ ἐφεῖτο. 'He (Lykourgos) did not allow them to engage in menial craft at all.'

Xenophon's reference here to 'the free men' must mean the Spartiates only. The perioikoi did not live 'in Sparta'; in the fourth century there were undoubtedly some men who were not slaves — disfranchised citizens, neodamodeis, and so on — who lived in Sparta and had to work for a living (compare Kinadon's count of people in the Agora, Xen. *Hell.* 3.3.5), but Xenophon has probably assumed that such men did not exist in the days of Lykourgos. His statement implies that slaves could and did undertake money-making activities, and no doubt the money thus made would go to their masters; Spartiates did not incur the taint of money-making if their slaves did menial work (the argument of Cartledge *LCM* 1 (1976) 118 goes astray here), but only if they did it with their own hands.

This topic, the single-minded devotion of the Spartans to military ends, is the one in which the moralizing and idealizing tendencies of both Xenophon and Plutarch are at their worst; nevertheless we can accept the assertion that Spartiates were not allowed to undertake menial work for profit. It is not refuted by the fact that there were certain skilled functions which Spartiates did perform (cf. Berthiaume *Mnemosyne* 29 (1976) 360-4). The functions of herald, piper, and cook were hereditary in certain families (Hdt. 6.60, 7.134.1); prophets, doctors, and pipers were among the king's entourage in war (Xen. *LP* 13.7). These are not to be regarded as professional men practising for profit. Each of them was the holder of a privilege (γέρας, Hdt. 7.134.1) which he exercised in addition to the normal military and other activities of a Spartiate — even the cook; for in this context the cook (μάγειρος, Hdt. 6.60) was surely not a servant who made soup for consumption every day, but a man who dealt with the animals sacrificed at public festivals.

Moralizing also affects Xenophon's and Plutarch's remarks on the currency. It is well known that the Spartans used iron bars or spits as money at a period when other cities had gold or silver coinage. This must have been a primitive survival, and both authors are undoubtedly wrong when they say that the Spartans had gold and silver coinage earlier and it was deliberately abolished to prevent avarice and luxury (Xen. *LP* 7.5, Plu. *Lyk.* 9.1-2). But there is no reason to reject the essential accuracy of Plutarch's account in his *Lysander*, indicating that a change occurred at the end of the Peloponnesian War; for that period he is likely to have had good evidence. He says that in 404 there was a great influx of gold and silver into Sparta, arising from the surplus of Persian subsidies for the war and gifts given by the cities which had formed the Athenian Empire, sent back to Sparta by Lysander. One distinguished general, Gylippos, was caught stealing some of it, and 'the most sensible of the Spartiates, led by this case in particular to fear the power of the money, on the ground that it was affecting citizens of no ordinary quality, reviled Lysander and called on the ephors to banish all the silver and gold as imported blights' (*Lys.* 17.2). The ephors put forward a proposal to do so, but friends of Lysander opposed it, and so a compromise was reached.

Plu. *Lys.* 17.6. δημοσίᾳ μὲν ἔδοξεν εἰσάγεσθαι νόμισμα τοιοῦτον, ἂν δέ τις ἁλῷ κεκτημένος ἰδίᾳ, ζημίαν ὥρισαν θάνατον. 'It was resolved that money of this kind be imported by the state, but if anyone was caught in private possession of it, they fixed death as the penalty.'

We should accept that this law prohibiting individuals from having gold or silver coins was made in 404 or shortly afterwards. (Cf. David *Sparta* 5-10. But David's statement that private possession of foreign coins was illegal before this date (p. 175, n.11) is incorrect; Plutarch makes clear that the ban imposed about 404 was a new one. Before that, presumably, acquisition of gold and silver coins by individuals occurred to only a modest extent, so that there was no need to prohibit it. When gold and silver were captured from the Persians in 479, no law prevented their distribution to individuals (Hdt. 9.81).) One man, named Thorax, was put to death for this offence (Plu. *Lys.* 19.7), and Xenophon confirms the existence of the law.

Xen. *LP* 7.6. χρυσίον γε μὴν καὶ ἀργύριον ἐρευνᾶται, καὶ ἄν τί που φανῇ, ὁ ἔχων ζημιοῦται. 'Gold and silver are sought out, and if any is found anywhere, the possessor is punished.'

But Xenophon adds later that this law is no longer observed (*LP* 14.3; for the bearing of this passage on the composition and date of *LP*, see page 9). In *Alkibiades 1*, a work of uncertain date doubtfully attributed to Plato, it is alleged that there is more gold and silver in private hands in Sparta than anywhere else in Greece (122e). Plutarch is firmly of the opinion that it was the acquisition of gold and silver after the defeat of Athens which made the Spartans self-indulgent and led to their decline (*Lyk.* 30.1, *Agis* 3.1, 5.1).

Probably the law prohibiting possession of gold and silver was not repealed, but was simply ignored.

MOURNING AND BURIAL OF THE DEAD

The final stage of an austere life was a discreet funeral. The main information about Spartan law on this subject is given by Plutarch. He first remarks that in Sparta, unlike many other Greek cities, there was no prohibition of burial within the city; the Spartans did not regard the dead as causing pollution, in the religious sense, to the living (*Lyk.* 27.1). The only three matters regulated by law were the burial of objects with the body, the inscription of the name on the tomb, and the period of mourning.

> Plu. *Lyk.* 27.2-4. συνθάπτειν οὐδὲν εἴασεν, ἀλλ' ἐν φοινικίδι καὶ φύλλοις ἐλαίας θέντες τὸ σῶμα περιέστελλον. ἐπιγράψαι δὲ τοὔνομα θάψαντας οὐκ ἐξῆν τοῦ νεκροῦ, πλὴν ἀνδρὸς ἐν πολέμῳ καὶ γυναικὸς †τῶν ἱερῶς† ἀποθανόντων. χρόνον δὲ πένθους ὀλίγον προσώρισεν, ἡμέρας ἕνδεκα· τῇ δὲ δωδεκάτῃ θύσαντας ἔδει Δήμητρι λύειν τὸ πένθος. 'He (Lykourgos) did not allow them to bury anything with the body, but they laid it out in a red cloak and olive leaves. When they buried it, it was not permitted to inscribe the name of the deceased, except for a man who died in war and a woman who died [text corrupt]. He fixed a short period of mourning, eleven days; on the twelfth they had to sacrifice to Demeter and end their mourning.'

These laws seem to be designed to prevent excessive displays of grief. The short period of mourning may be contrasted with the period of thirty days which appears to have been normal in Athens (Lys. 1.14, Harp. under τριακάς). Other Greeks sometimes had valuable possessions buried with them: in Sparta the red cloak was the soldier's uniform (Xen. *LP* 11.3), and the point of burying him in it was surely that he valued no possession more highly than his membership of the Spartan army. (If that explanation is right, this item in Plutarch's account will not have been applicable to women.) We should not take Plutarch as meaning that the burial of the red cloak with its owner was compulsory, but only that it was permitted although other valuable objects were forbidden. Aelian says that a man was buried in leaves if he died after fighting well, in a red cloak only if he had performed deeds of special distinction (*Var. Hist.* 6.6).

As for the law about epitaphs, how should we cure the corruption in Plutarch's text? τῶν ἱερῶς ἀποθανόντων, 'those (men and women) who died in a holy manner', seems impossible. One good manuscript offers τῶν ἱερῶν ἀποθανόντων, 'the holy (men and women) who died'. Den Boer *Laconian Studies* 294-300 defends this, as meaning that only priests, if killed in war, and priestesses could have their names inscribed on their tombs. It could be right; yet it is not wholly satisfactory, because the normal words for a priest and priestess are ἱερεύς and ἱέρεια, and because the arrangement of Plutarch's sentence makes us expect an epithet with γυναικός, corresponding to ἐν πολέμῳ with ἀνδρός. Recent editors (Ziegler, Flacelière, Manfredini and Piccirilli) adopt a bold conjecture by Latte: [τῶν] λεχοῦς ἀποθανόντων, giving the sense 'except for a man who died in war and a woman who died in childbirth'. The evidence supporting this conjecture consists of the inscriptions on Spartan tombs of a later period: several for men give a name with the phrase ἐν πολέμῳ (*IG* 5(1) 701-10), while one for a woman says Ἀγιππία λεχόι and another with the name lost says . . .] λεχόι (*IG* 5(1) 713-14). A rule which reserves the greatest honour for a man who has died in war or a woman who has died in childbirth fits perfectly with the Spartan principle that a man's aim in life is to be a good soldier and a woman's to be the mother of good soldiers. Thus den Boer is wrong to say that Latte's conjecture is 'without justification'; it gives precisely the sense required, and so it should be accepted, even though it is not clear how λεχοῦς became corrupted to τῶν ἱερῶς.

None of these restrictions on extravagant mourning applied to the death of a king. Herodotos describes elaborate lamentation for kings, and Xenophon remarks that they were honoured not as human beings but as heroes (Hdt. 6.58, Xen. *LP* 15.9, *Hell.* 3.3.1).

VII

The Administration of Justice

JUDGES

The Spartans knew nothing of the modern theory that the judiciary should be separate from executive officers. The principal judges were the same as the principal officers of government: the two kings (βασιλεῖς), the twenty-eight senators (γέροντες), and the five ephors (ἔφοροι). Only their judicial functions will be considered here; for their other functions readers should consult works on the Spartan constitution.

The kings by themselves judged only three kinds of case, according to Hdt. 6.57.4-5 (quoted on page 96): those concerning the marriage of heiresses, public roads, and adoption. Heiresses and adoption have been discussed in Chapter V. We know nothing else about cases concerning roads; presumably they were cases in which someone was accused of ploughing up or otherwise obstructing a right of way. We are also not told why these particular kinds of case were reserved for the kings, but we can guess that before the institution of the ephors the kings' judicial powers were much more extensive, or even unlimited, and the cases listed by Herodotos were those which remained to them after most were transferred to the ephors. In the classical period it was normal for one king to go out on campaigns while the other stayed at home (Hdt. 5.75.2); when both were in Sparta they may have judged jointly, but when one was away the other must have acted as sole judge.

But Herodotos's list may be less complete than he claims. Aristotle's statement that religious matters (τὰ πρὸς τοὺς θεούς) were given to the kings (*Pol.* 1285a 6-7) may be taken to include judging disputes about religious requirements. But the kings' most extensive judicial powers were probably those which they exercised on military campaigns; here, however, there are difficulties in the evidence.

Xen. *LP* 13.11. ἢν δ' οὖν δίκης δεόμενός τις ἔλθῃ, πρὸς ἑλλανοδίκας τοῦτον ὁ βασιλεὺς ἀποπέμπει. 'But if anyone comes requesting justice, the king sends him off to the hellanodikai.'

Plu. *Ages.* 7.6-7. ἔπειτα τῶν ἐντυγχανόντων καὶ δεομένων οὓς αἴσθοιτο Λυσάνδρῳ μάλιστα πεποιθότας, ἀπράκτους ἀπέπεμπε· καὶ περὶ τὰς κρίσεις ὁμοίως, οἷς ἐκεῖνος ἐπηρεάζοι, τούτους ἔδει πλέον ἔχοντας ἀπελθεῖν, καὶ τοὐναντίον, οὓς φανερὸς γένοιτο προθυμούμενος ὠφελεῖν, χαλεπὸν ἦν μὴ καὶ ζημιωθῆναι. 'Secondly, of those who met him (Agesilaos) and addressed requests to him, he dismissed with a refusal whoever he saw relying most on Lysander; and concerning judgements likewise, any men whom Lysander treated scornfully were bound to come off victorious, while on the other hand any whom he was obviously keen to assist had difficulty in avoiding being actually punished.'

Plutarch is recounting the successful efforts of the young king Agesilaos to take Lysander down a peg during his campaign in Asia. The first half of his sentence refers to petitions and requests for favours, like Xen. *Hell.* 3.4.8 in another account of the same period, but the second half clearly distinguishes from the requests trials which might result in penalties. In the circumstances of the army in Asia they cannot have been trials concerning heiresses, adoption, or public roads; Plutarch means that the king decided cases of other kinds in the field. How can that be reconciled with the statement in Xen. *LP* 13.11 that the king sent cases to the hellanodikai for trial? Xenophon personally served under Agesilaos and cannot be wrong on this point. There is no other evidence about Spartan officials called hellanodikai, but from their name, which appears to mean 'judges for Greeks' (compare the xenodikai and nautodikai in Athens), we may guess that they tried cases involving Greeks other than Lakedaimonians. We can accept both Xenophon's and Plutarch's evidence if we take Xenophon as meaning that the hellanodikai dealt with disputes between a Lakedaimonian and an alien, and Plutarch as meaning that the king decided disputes between Lakedaimonians when they were abroad on campaigns. That is better than simply discarding Plutarch's evidence as a mistake, because Aristotle too associates the king with military justice. But here further difficulty arises from corruption in the text.

> Arist. *Pol.* 1285a 7-10. αὕτη μὲν οὖν ἡ βασιλεία οἷον στρατηγία τις αὐτοκρατόρων καὶ ἀίδιός ἐστιν· κτεῖναι γὰρ οὐ κύριος, εἰ μὴ †ἔν τινι βασιλείᾳ†, καθάπερ ἐπὶ τῶν ἀρχαίων ἐν ταῖς πολεμικαῖς ἐξόδοις, ἐν χειρὸς νόμῳ. δηλοῖ δ' Ὅμηρος ... 'This (Spartan) kingship is like a generalship with powers of independent decision, of indefinite duration. He does not have authority to put anyone to death, except [text corrupt], just as in campaigns of war in ancient times, by the law of physical force. Homer shows this ...'

Aristotle goes on to quote the *Iliad*, in which Agamemnon has to submit to criticism in the assemblies but can kill on the spot any coward whom he sees running away in battle. This makes clear the point of the phrase 'except...', even though it is doubtful which of the various emendations proposed should be accepted (ἔν τινι καιρῷ Richards: ἕνεκα δειλίας Bywater: perhaps ἐν λιποταξίᾳ might be considered): the Spartan king had authority to execute on the spot a deserter in battle. Otherwise he did not have authority to impose the death penalty, but the manner in which Aristotle mentions this limitation of his power seems to imply that he did have authority to impose lesser penalties on campaigns, and thus confirms the evidence of Plutarch.

Because they reigned for life, most kings eventually became very experienced. But they often began young, and the chances of having a youthful king were increased by the curious law of succession, which laid down that a son born after his father became king took precedence over one born before (Hdt. 7.3.3). So there must often have been a remarkable contrast between the kings and the senators, who had to be over sixty years old (Plu. *Lyk*. 26.1). Candidates for the senate used to canvass for election, and the method of election, which Aristotle regards as childish, was that those who received the loudest shouting in their favour at a meeting of the assembly were successful (Arist. *Pol*. 1271a 9-18, Plu. *Lyk*. 26.3-5). It must have been primarily a popularity contest, though Aristotle in another passage implies that the election was δυναστευτική, 'based on power' (*Pol*. 1306a 18-19). That word is vague; it may mean that the citizens tended to support candidates who had already held power as ephors or polemarchs, but perhaps a better interpretation is that they supported those whose fathers had been senators, so that certain families were senatorial by tradition (cf. Finley

Use 169-70 = *Econ. and Soc.* 32-3, de Ste. Croix *Origins* 353-4). Even so, the method of election surely favoured men of some merit, and the qualification which our sources emphasize is moral virtue, not birth or property (Xen. *LP* 10.1-3, Arist. *Pol.* 1270b 24-5, Plu. *Lyk.* 26.2). The Spartan senators must have been better judges than members of the Areopagos in Athens, who after 487 were in effect picked by lottery.

Once elected, the senators remained in office for life, and were not answerable to anyone for their decisions; in Athenian terminology, they were ἀνεύθυνοι (Arist. *Pol.* 1271a 5-6). The two kings, even when young, were included in the senate *ex officio*, making a total body of thirty. When a king was absent, the senator most nearly related to him voted on the king's behalf as well as his own; so much seems clear from a sentence in Herodotos which is otherwise confused or corrupt (6.57.5; cf. Richards *Xenophon* 227-8, Gomme *HCT* 1.137-8).

The senate was the supreme court of law. It tried cases in which the penalty was death or exile or disfranchisement (Xen. *LP* 10.2, Plu. *Lyk.* 26.2; and in Arist. *Pol.* 1294b 33-4 the 'few' who control the penalties of death and exile can be taken to be the senate, because the senators are identified in 1265b 37-8 as the oligarchic part of the constitution). These included cases of homicide (Arist. *Pol.* 1275b 10). It is not known which other offences, if any, were referred to the senate automatically. It may have been within the discretion of the ephors to decide that a particular case should go to the senate, if they thought it was serious enough to require one of the penalties which only the senate could impose. Probably only trials of Spartiates went to the senate. The ephors could impose the death penalty on perioikoi (Isok. 12.181, quoted on page 30); and they probably imposed it on Kinadon, who was a free non-citizen resident in Sparta. (Xen. *Hell.* 3.3.11 is not quite clear about that trial, but the ephors must be the subject of συνελάμβανον, and should therefore be understood as the subject of τέλος αὐτὸν ἤροντο ..., in which the word τέλος makes clear that the reference is to the final stage of trial, just before the penalty was imposed.) Two passages in Plutarch might be taken to imply that the ephors could condemn a Spartiate to death. One is an anecdote in the collection of apophthegms, in which a man named Thektamenes was condemned to death by the ephors (Plu. *Eth.* 221f); but the text does not say that he was a Spartiate. In the other we read that the ephors 'arrested one Thorax, who was in private possession of silver, and put him to death' (Plu. *Lys.* 19.7); perhaps that is a loose way of saying that they got him condemned by the senate (there is a comparable instance of ἀποκτείνειν in Lys. 30.11). These two passages create some doubt, but on the whole it seems more likely that only the senate could impose the death penalty on a Spartiate.

According to Pausanias, when a king was to be tried, the judges included the ephors along with the senators and the other king.

> Paus. 3.5.2. βασιλεῖ δὲ τῷ Λακεδαιμονίων δικαστήριον ἐκάθιζον οἵ τε ὀνομαζόμενοι γέροντες, ὀκτὼ καὶ εἴκοσιν ὄντες ἀριθμόν, καὶ ἡ τῶν ἐφόρων ἀρχή, σὺν δὲ αὐτοῖς καὶ ὁ τῆς οἰκίας βασιλεὺς τῆς ἑτέρας. 'As a court to try a king of the Lakedaimonians, the so-called senators, who were twenty-eight in number, and the board of ephors sat together with the king of the other house.'

It has been assumed that the court for all criminal cases included the ephors in addition to the kings and the senators (Bonner and Smith *CP* 37 (1942) 113). But there is no clear evidence for that, and Pausanias's words rather imply that such a court was a special one, used only when a king was the defendant. Possibly it seemed appropriate to include the ephors then because the senate would otherwise have been below normal strength (with one king excluded from it) and because checking the kings was a traditional function of the ephors.

Normally we hear of the ephors judging separately from the senate. The five ephors were also elected from the Spartiates, but they did not have to be over sixty, and they held office for only one year (cf. Westlake *GRBS* 17 (1976) 343-52, Rhodes *Historia* 30 (1981) 498-502). As Aristotle points out, they were just ordinary men, with no special qualifications (*Pol.* 1270b 28-31, quoted on page 130). Yet their competence was very extensive.

Xen. *LP* 8.4. ἔφοροι οὖν ἱκανοὶ μέν εἰσι ζημιοῦν ὃν ἂν βούλωνται, κύριοι δ' ἐκπράττειν παραχρῆμα, κύριοι δὲ καὶ ἄρχοντας μεταξὺ καταπαῦσαι καὶ εἷρξαί γε καὶ περὶ τῆς ψυχῆς εἰς ἀγῶνα καταστῆσαι. τοσαύτην δὲ ἔχοντες δύναμιν οὐχ ὥσπερ αἱ ἄλλαι πόλεις ἐῶσι τοὺς αἱρεθέντας ἀεὶ ἄρχειν τὸ ἔτος ὅπως ἂν βούλωνται, ἀλλ' ὥσπερ οἱ τύραννοι καὶ οἱ ἐν τοῖς γυμνικοῖς ἀγῶσιν ἐπιστάται, ἤν τινα αἰσθάνωνται παρανομοῦντά τι, εὐθὺς παραχρῆμα κολάζουσι. 'The ephors are competent to punish whoever they wish, and they have authority to exact payment forthwith. They also have authority to dismiss officials during their term of office, and even to imprison them and to put them on trial for their lives. Having such power they do not, like other cities, allow those who have been elected each year to rule however they like throughout the year, but, like tyrants and umpires at athletic contests, if they notice anyone doing anything illegal they punish him immediately.'

Their competence 'to punish whoever they wish' gave them extraordinarily wide discretion: they could decide for themselves what conduct they wanted to punish, regardless of whether there was any law or general opinion about it. It is not surprising that this feature of the system is one which Aristotle criticizes.

> Arist. *Pol.* 1270b 28-31. ἔτι δὲ καὶ κρίσεών εἰσι μεγάλων κύριοι, ὄντες οἱ τυχόντες, διόπερ οὐκ αὐτογνώμονας βέλτιον κρίνειν ἀλλὰ κατὰ γράμματα καὶ τοὺς νόμους. 'Besides they also have authority to make important judgements, although they are ordinary men, so that it would be better for them not to judge by their own opinions but in accordance with written rules and the laws.'

The question arises whether each ephor could exercise this power individually or only the whole board acting together. The latter arrangement would reduce the risk of verdicts given by personal whim or spite. But there were at least some cases which individual ephors judged.

> Arist. *Pol.* 1275b 9-10. ἐν Λακεδαίμονι τὰς τῶν συμβολαίων δικάζει τῶν ἐφόρων ἄλλος ἄλλας. 'In Lakedaimon individual ephors try different cases of contracts.'

'Contract' may be a misleading translation of συμβόλαιον. The word is not restricted to formal agreements, still less to written agreements, which were probably rare in Sparta. It can be used of any relationship between persons in which one has a liability to the other (cf. W. Wyse's note on Isaios 4.12, H. J. Wolff *Die attische Paragraphe* (1966) 44 n.56). Thus Aristotle may well be referring here to private cases of all kinds, just as in Athens the subjects of δίκαι ἴδιαι were τὰ τοῦ καθ' ἡμέραν βίου συμβόλαια (Dem. 18.210). The vagueness of the word leaves the point uncertain; we can say only that a single ephor judged a private case of some kinds, and perhaps of all kinds. One of the collection of apophthegms tells us that such cases were tried every day, and its phrase 'among enemies' means that this function was performed also by the ephors who accompanied the army on campaigns.

> Plu. *Eth.* 221a-b. Εὐρυκρατίδας ὁ Ἀναξανδρίδου, πυνθανομένου τινὸς διὰ τί τὰ περὶ τῶν συμβολαίων δίκαια ἑκάστης ἡμέρας κρίνουσιν οἱ ἔφοροι, "ὅπως" ἔφη "καὶ ἐν τοῖς πολεμίοις πιστεύωμεν ἀλλήλοις". 'Eurykratidas son of Anaxandridas, when someone asked why the ephors judged cases concerning contracts every day, said "So that we may trust one another even among enemies".'

On the other hand, it is hard to believe that Xen. *LP* 8.4 means that every ephor had authority individually to dismiss any other magistrate. Aristotle attributes the power over other magistrates to ἡ τῶν ἐφόρων ἀρχή (*Pol.* 1271a 6), and this probably means the whole board of ephors. And in other public affairs we hear of 'the ephors' taking action. For example, Kleomenes I 'went to the ephors' to complain about the activities of Maiandrios of Samos, 'and they in response banished Maiandrios' (Hdt. 3.148.2); when he returned from his expedition to Argos, 'his enemies took him before the ephors' to accuse him (Hdt. 6.82.1); an informer revealed the conspiracy of Kinadon to 'the ephors', and 'the ephors' questioned him and took subsequent action (Xen. *Hell.* 3.3.4-11). So it seems likely that in public cases the ephors judged jointly, not individually, although we are not able to say exactly how the distinction between public and private cases was defined. Probably a majority vote was decisive and unanimity was not required; at least, king Pausanias obtained a decision 'persuading three of the ephors' (Xen. *Hell.* 2.4.29), though that was a decision to take military action and it is possible that judicial verdicts were different. When two of the ephors were away on a campaign (Xen. *LP* 13.5, *Hell.* 2.4.36), the three remaining in Sparta must have been able to act for the whole board; whether the two with the army could also act for the whole board, no evidence shows.

There is also a little evidence for judicial activity by the kings and ephors together. When the wife of king Ariston gave birth to a baby, one of his servants brought him the news 'while he was sitting on a bench with the ephors' (Hdt. 6.63.2); and in 369 king Agesilaos 'after consultation with the ephors' put some conspirators to death (Plu. *Ages.* 32.11). However, this action of Agesilaos was certainly illegal; it was justified only by the emergency, because 'it was impracticable to try them amid such confusion' as Plutarch says in the preceding sentence. As for Ariston, Herodotos does not say what he and the ephors were doing on a bench ($\dot{\epsilon}\nu\ \theta\dot{\omega}\kappa\wp$); in the context the point is merely that the ephors were near enough to overhear Ariston's comment 'It can't be mine'. The ephors had chairs ($\delta\dot{\iota}\phi\rho o\iota$) as their official seats (Xen. *LP* 15.6, Plu. *Agis* 12.4, *Kleom.* 10.1), and the bench could have been, for example, a bench for spectators at a festival. So this evidence is inadequate to prove that any cases were judged by the kings and ephors together, without the senators.

Very little is known about judicial activities by any other magistrates. Mention has already been made of the magistrate who judged cases on Kythera (pages 29-30) and of the hellanodikai (pages 124-5). There is no evidence about the hellanodikai other than the passage about the kings on campaigns (Xen. *LP* 13.11). It may be that those magistrates tried cases arising between a Lakedaimonian and an alien in

THE ADMINISTRATION OF JUSTICE

Sparta itself as well as on campaigns abroad; but since foreigners were discouraged from visiting Sparta, perhaps few such cases arose there. It is also possible that the Spartan judges sent to try the defeated Plataians in 427 and the captured Ismenias of Thebes in 382 were hellanodikai, but the historians do not say so (Thuc. 3.52.3, Xen. *Hell.* 5.2.35).

The transmitted text of Plu. *Lyk.* 12.5 says that the polemarchs (πολέμαρχοι) imposed a penalty on king Agis II, but that must be wrong. The same anecdote appears among the apophthegms attributed to Agis (no.6 in Plu. *Eth.* 226f-227a), with almost the same wording, except that there the penalty is attributed to the ephors. We should regard that as the earlier version (cf. page 22); when the anecdote was later incorporated into *Lyk.* 12.5, Plutarch (or a copyist) carelessly failed to insert the words οἱ ἔφοροι. So there is no good evidence for judicial activity by the polemarchs.

Inscriptions of the Roman period mention Spartan officials called πατρονόμοι and νομοφύλακες (*IG* 5(1) 18b, 32b, etc.). But the πατρονόμοι were instituted only by Kleomenes III in the third century (Paus. 2.9.1). When the νομοφύλακες were instituted is not known, but there is no evidence of their existence in the period with which this book is concerned.

Finally there is the question whether the whole assembly of Spartan citizens ever tried a case. Herodotos sometimes refers to a verdict given by 'the Spartiates' or 'the Lakedaimonians'. However, that does not necessarily mean the assembly, as one of the instances makes clear.

> Hdt. 6.85.1. Λακεδαιμόνιοι δὲ δικαστήριον συναγαγόντες ἔγνωσαν περιυβρίσθαι Αἰγινήτας ὑπὸ Λευτυχίδεω. 'The Lakedaimonians convened a court and decided that the Aiginetans had been treated outrageously by Leotykhidas.'

In this case the verdict was that of a court, evidently the court constituted for trial of a king (the senators, the ephors, and the other king), acting on behalf of the state. Strictly, it was those thirty-four men (or a majority of them) who decided the verdict, and probably only the five ephors who convened the court; but even within the one sentence 'the Lakedaimonians' refers to both of those bodies, meaning that each action was taken by those Spartans who had authority to take it. Thus in a Thucydidean passage, where 'the Lakedaimonians' are said to have imposed a verdict on Agis II and later passed a law (Thuc. 5.63), that does not necessarily mean that both actions were taken by the same body, and it is an oversimplification to say 'If the Spartans are passing a law, we are dealing with the assembly' (Lewis *Sparta and Persia* 39). Various organs of state performed various functions, and each was, in its due place, 'the Lakedaimonians'.

If, then, 'the Spartiates' or 'the Lakedaimonians' can mean simply 'the proper Spartan court', we are left with no evidence that the assembly ever tried cases, except for two in which the kingship itself was the subject of dispute. The first was the one by which Leotykhidas supplanted Demaratos. The second was the one by which Agesilaos successfully claimed the kingship from a later Leotykhidas.

> Hdt. 6.66.1. τέλος δὲ ἐόντων περὶ αὐτῶν νεικέων ἔδοξε Σπαρτιήτῃσι ἐπείρεσθαι τὸ χρηστήριον τὸ ἐν Δελφοῖσι εἰ Ἀρίστωνος εἴη παῖς ὁ Δημάρητος. 'Finally quarrels broke out about them, and the Spartiates decided to ask the oracle at Delphi whether Demaratos was the son of Ariston.'

> Xen. *Hell*. 3.3.4. τοιαῦτα δὲ ἀκούσασα ἡ πόλις ἀμφοτέρων Ἀγησίλαον εἴλοντο βασιλέα. 'After the city

THE ADMINISTRATION OF JUSTICE

had heard such arguments as these from both sides, they chose Agesilaos to be king.'

In the first of these cases the quarrels and the failure to reach a verdict do not sound like the proceedings of the senate. In the second it seems unlikely that Xenophon would call the senate 'the city' (despite the acceptance of this possibility by de Ste. Croix *Origins* 351). So probably in both cases the ephors referred to the assembly the question 'Who shall be king?' This was, after all, a very rare kind of question, and should perhaps not be regarded as a trial at all. But these two were not quite the only instances of it. In the third century Kleonymos and Areus disputed the kingship, and that dispute was decided by the senators (Paus. 3.6.2).

There is no other evidence for trial by the assembly, and against it is the statement of Aristotle that cases were tried by various ἀρχαί, 'authorities' (*Pol.* 1275b 7-12; cf. de Ste. Croix *Origins* 349-50). When the mother and grandmother of Agis IV cried that he should be tried by the citizens (Plu. *Agis* 19.10), their demand was contrary to Spartan tradition and precedent.

PROSECUTIONS AND TRIALS

Virtually all the surviving accounts of individual trials in Sparta concern public cases of national importance. About the procedure in private cases we can only make guesses. We have already seen that some, perhaps all, private cases were tried by a single ephor (pages 130-1). When two individuals had a dispute, presumably one of them would apply to the ephors for trial. Since the ephors held trials every day (Plu. *Eth.* 221a-b, quoted on page 131), perhaps application could be made on any day. It is not known how a particular ephor was selected for a particular case, nor how the defendant was summoned to appear. No doubt the ephor heard both the prosecutor and the defendant speak, together with any witnesses whom they produced, and then gave his verdict. Since Spartans were notoriously short of speech, the Athenian device of the water-clock for limiting the length of speeches will not have been required.

Arbitration could be used to avoid the need for trial by an ephor. One of the apophthegms attributed to king Arkhidamos II concerns an arbitration.

> Plu. *Eth.* 218d. δύο δέ τινων διαιτητὴν αὐτὸν λαβόντων, ἀγαγὼν εἰς τὸ τῆς Χαλκιοίκου τέμενος ἐξώρκισεν ἐμμεῖναι τοῖς κριθεῖσιν αὐτούς· ὁμοσάντων δ' ἐκείνων "κρίνω τοίνυν" ἔφη "μὴ πρότερον ἀπελθεῖν ὑμᾶς ἐκ τοῦ τεμένους, πρὶν ἂν τὰ πρὸς ἀλλήλους διαλύσησθε". 'When two men took him as arbitrator, he led them into the precinct of the Brazen-house goddess and made them swear to abide by his decisions. When they had sworn, he said "Well then, my decision is that you are not to leave the precinct until you have made up your quarrel".'

Probably this arbitration was just a private arrangement. It does not prove that in Sparta, as in many private cases in Athens, the parties were required to present their evidence to a publicly appointed arbitrator before they could proceed to a formal trial. Still less does it prove that all arbitrations were held in the precinct of Athena of the Brazen-house, or that it was standard procedure to forbid the parties to leave until their quarrel was settled; some modern writers have missed the joke (Bonner and Smith *CP* 37 (1942) 127, Michell *Sparta* 154). We do not know whether any procedure at all was laid down by law for arbitrations.

In public cases, in which the interests of the state as a whole

THE ADMINISTRATION OF JUSTICE

were involved, it is clear that all preliminary proceedings were in the hands of the ephors. If they discovered anyone doing something which they considered wrong, they took action on their own initiative (Xen. *LP* 8.4, quoted on page 129). Alternatively anyone could give information or make an accusation to the ephors (e.g. Hdt. 6.82.1). The ephors might then make investigations in a manner which we should regard as appropriate for police rather than for magistrates. The case of Kinadon is one which is recorded in some detail: when the ephors received information about a conspiracy, they interrogated the informer, and then, after consultation with some of the senators, they made a secret plan for Kinadon to be arrested on a journey to Aulon, interrogated, and brought back to Sparta for trial (Xen. *Hell.* 3.3.4-11). Perhaps the most extraordinary detective investigation carried out by ephors was that of Pausanias the regent: it involved building in the precinct at Tainaron a hut divided by a partition, behind which the ephors hid and eavesdropped on a conversation between Pausanias and his servant to obtain evidence of his guilt (Thuc. 1.133). If they thought fit, they could arrest and imprison anyone, even a king (Thuc. 1.131.2).

When the ephors, besides detecting or investigating the offence, were also the judges, the trial must sometimes have been hardly more than a formality. Presumably the accused was allowed to speak in his own defence, and perhaps to call on others as witnesses or speakers in his support; but the judges must often have made up their minds in advance, and one may sympathize with the view of Isokrates that a trial by the ephors was no trial at all (12.181, quoted on page 30). However, the most serious cases required trial by the senate. (On the question which cases went to the senate, see pages 127-8.)

Part of a fragment found in a Vatican palimpsest seems to refer to investigation by the ephors before a trial by the senate. It was published first by Aly *Frag. Vat.* and more recently by Keaney *TAPA* 104 (1974) 179-94. Aly believed that it referred to examination of magistrates, but Keaney has shown convincingly that it is about trial procedures, and has plausibly suggested that it comes from the lost *Laws* of Theophrastos; A. Szegedy-Maszak places it in an appendix to his edition of the fragments of that work. It discusses the merits of various procedures in general, but Sparta is mentioned as an example at several points. (I give Aly's and Keaney's text, but without using brackets or dotted letters to mark restorations or corrections of only one or two letters.)

Vat. Gr. 2306 fr. A 1-30. [... ἐὰν κατ' ἐξετασ]μόν, ὅπερ καὶ διαιτητὴς ποιεῖ χρόνιον ὂν καὶ ἐργῶδες, ἕκαστον ἀνακρίνῃ, καθάπερ ἐν Λακεδαίμονι ποιοῦσιν· διὸ κρεῖττον ἴσως ἄτε τὸ ἀκριβὲς ζητοῦντας πολλὰς ἀδικάστους ποιεῖν ἢ ἄνευ τῆς ἀνακρίσεως δικάζειν, ἐπεὶ καὶ τοῦτο πλεονεξίαν [τινὰ] ποιεῖ τοῖς φιλονικοῦσιν, ὅπερ φασὶ συμβαίνειν καὶ ἐν τῇ Σπάρτῃ. τοιγὰρ σκυτάλῃ ἀνακρίνουσιν οὕτως καὶ ἀνακρίναντες ἐκκαλοῦσιν τῇ ὥρᾳ τοὺς ἄλλους, ὃ καὶ Κλεομένης ἐποίησεν ὁ βασιλεὺς ἐν τῇ κρίσει τῇ ἐς Κλεόλαν. '... if by an examination, as an arbitrator does, although it is a long and arduous task, he questions each man, just as they do in Lakedaimon. Therefore it is perhaps better, in seeking the exact truth, to leave many (cases) untried than to try them without the questioning, since that gives an advantage to the argumentative — which they say happens even in Sparta. That is why they question in that way, with a *skytale*, and after the questioning convene the other men

THE ADMINISTRATION OF JUSTICE

at the due time, as king Kleomenes did too in the trial for Kleolas.'

The words ἀδικάστους and δικάζειν make it reasonable to assume that the feminine noun to be understood with πολλάς is δίκας, and that the whole passage is about trials. The lost subject of ἀνακρίνῃ must be ὁ ἄρχων or something similar, and the point of the passage is that a just verdict is more likely to be obtained if the magistrate conducts a thorough interrogation to elicit all relevant evidence before the trial proper; that leaves less scope for obfuscation of facts by rhetoric. (τοῖς φιλονικοῦσιν, which perhaps ought to be written -νεικ-, refers to men who like arguing.) The noun and verb ἀνάκρισις and ἀνακρίνω are general words for questioning and do not necessarily have a technical sense, but in Athens there was an official part of the judicial procedure with the name ἀνάκρισις (e.g. Isaios 6.12-13) in which the magistrate put questions to the litigants to clarify the nature of the charge and the defence. However, Theophrastos refers not to Athens but to Sparta for his example. That is probably because Sparta offered the best example of very thorough interrogation by magistrates, covering not just the clarification of the charge but all the details of the case. Theophrastos must be thinking primarily of the investigation by the ephors before convening the senate for the trial of a case in which the penalty would be death or exile or disfranchisement; τοὺς ἄλλους must mean the senators. A few details remain obscure. It is uncertain how a *skytale* was used for trials; but in other contexts a *skytale* is a device for written messages and records, and so probably here the meaning is that the questions and answers at the ephors' interrogation were recorded in writing for presentation at the trial (cf. Keaney *TAPA* 104 (1974) 191 n.29). Nothing is known about the case of Kleomenes and Kleolas, in which the interrogation appears to have been conducted by the king instead of the ephors. This was probably Kleomenes I, who was a strong character and tended to act independently of the ephors (e.g. Hdt. 5.49-51), rather than Kleomenes II (as suggested by Aly *Frag. Vat.* 33). The word καί indicates that the case was exceptional, and the passage should not be taken as evidence that interrogation by a king was the correct legal procedure.

Trials by the senate will not have been very frequent. Presumably the ephors requested a sitting of the senate when they had an accused person for trial. A phrase in Plutarch implies that they issued a written notice of the trial, including the proposed penalty: κρίσιν προγράψαι θανατικήν, 'to give written notice of a capital trial' (*Lys.* 30.1). But there is no evidence for the suggestion that the ephors presided at the trial (Bonner and Smith *CP* 37 (1942) 124); it is not known who acted as chairman of the senators. The accused stood before them in bonds of some kind, according to an anecdote about the suppression by Herippidas of disorder in the Spartan colony of Herakleia in Trakhinia.

> Polyain. *Strat.* 2.21. ὁ δὲ ἐκέλευσεν αὐτούς, περὶ ὧν ἀδικοῦσι, Λακεδαιμονίοις κρίσιν ὑποσχεῖν, ὡς νόμιμόν ἐστιν ἐν τῇ Σπαρτιάτιδι, δεθέντας. 'He ordered them to undergo trial by the Lakedaimonians for their offences, bound, as is the rule in Sparta.'

In some cases the ephors must have been the prosecutors. But when an accusation had been made by someone else, no doubt the accuser spoke at the trial. The accused could also speak; king Kleomenes I, for example, made a long speech to defend himself (Hdt. 6.82). Xen. *Hell.* 3.3.2-3 reports a debate between Agesilaos and Leotykhidas, followed by a supporting speaker on each side; but that may have been at a meeting of the assembly rather than a trial by the senate (see pages 134-5). Many Spartans were not good orators, and sometimes the accused may have done little more than answer the questions put to him by the senators. That is what seems to have happened at the trial of king Agis IV; however, that trial in the third century was held in the prison with not all the senators present, and is not a reliable guide to the correct legal procedure in the classical period (Plu. *Agis* 19.5-8). It was even possible for a trial to proceed without the accused speaking or attending at all: when Sphodrias was accused after his unauthorized attempt to seize Peiraieus, he was afraid of condemnation and stayed away from the trial, but in the event he was acquitted (Xen. *Hell.* 5.4.24, Plu. *Ages.* 24.9-26.1). In Athens, if a defendant was absent without proper reason, a verdict was given against him automatically; but in Sparta, as the case of Sphodrias shows, a full trial could be held in his absence.

In two trials of kings we find that the verdict was decided by majority vote.

> Hdt. 6.82.2. ταῦτα δὲ λέγων πιστά τε καὶ οἰκότα ἐδόκεε Σπαρτιήτῃσι λέγειν καὶ ἀπέφυγε πολλὸν τοὺς διώκοντας. 'This speech which he (Kleomenes I) made seemed to the Spartiates to be convincing and reasonable, and he was acquitted by a large majority over the prosecutors.'

> Paus. 3.5.2. τέσσαρες μὲν δὴ καὶ δέκα τῶν γερόντων, ἐπὶ δὲ αὐτοῖς Ἆγις ὁ τῆς ἑτέρας οἰκίας βασιλεύς, ἀδικεῖν τὸν Παυσανίαν κατέγνωσαν· τὸ δὲ ἄλλο ἀπέγνω δικαστήριον. 'Fourteen of the senators, and in addition to them Agis, the king of the other house, gave a verdict of

guilty against Pausanias; but the rest of the court gave a verdict in his favour.'

The reference to the king's vote in the latter passage shows that it was known how individuals had voted; the voting was not secret. But the method of voting is not known. It is also unknown whether a second vote was used, as in many cases in Athens, to decide the penalty. There is some evidence that the senators took several days to decide the penalty. It consists of one of the apophthegms attributed to Anaxandridas II, together with an incomplete phrase in the Vatican palimpsest already mentioned.

> Plu. *Eth.* 217a-b. ἐρωτῶντος δέ τινος αὐτὸν διὰ τί τὰς περὶ θανάτου δίκας πλείοσιν ἡμέραις οἱ γέροντες κρίνουσι, κἂν ἀποφύγῃ τις, οὐδὲν ἧσσόν ἐστιν ὑπόδικος, "πολλαῖς μὲν ἡμέραις" ἔφη "κρίνουσιν, ὅτι περὶ θανάτου τοῖς διαμαρτάνουσιν οὐκ ἔστι μεταβουλεύσασθαι· νόμῳ δ' ὑπόδικον δεήσει εἶναι, διότι κατὰ τοῦτον τὸν νόμον ἂν εἴη καὶ τὸ κρείττονα βουλεύσασθαι". 'When someone asked him why the senators judge capital cases on several days, and, if a man is acquitted, he is nonetheless subject to prosecution, he said "They judge on a number of days because those who make a mistake about death cannot change their decision; and he must be subject to prosecution by law because this law makes it possible to change the decision for the better".'

> Vat. Gr. 2306 fr. A 44-7. [... πολλὰς] ἡμέρας ἀκροᾶσθαι καθάπερ [ἐν] Λακεδαίμονι. '... to hear for a number of days, as in Lakedaimon.'

A reference in Plato to 'other people' who take several days over a judgement concerning death (*Apol.* 37a) probably relates to Sparta. But it is difficult to believe that the

THE ADMINISTRATION OF JUSTICE

speeches and presentation of evidence lasted several days. (In Athens, where loquacity was surely commoner, no trial took more than one day.) It is more likely that, if the penalty proposed was death, the court was adjourned and met again several days later, so that the senators could discuss the case again, and perhaps question the defendant further, after they had had time to think it over. There may even have been two or more adjournments (since πολλαῖς ἡμέραις implies sittings on more than two days) before they finally confirmed the death penalty.

The second point mentioned in the apophthegm of Anaxandridas is also confirmed by the Vatican palimpsest in a later sentence.

> Vat. Gr. 2306 fr. A 69-77. ἐνίων δὲ κἂν ἀποφύγῃ πολλάκις ἀκροασαμένων καὶ ἀνακρινάντων, ὁσίως ὑπεύθυνόν πως πάλιν ποιητέον ὥσπερ ἐν Λακεδαί[μον]ι.
> 'When some (judges) have heard and questioned him, even if he does get acquitted, he ought to be made subject to examination again in some sanctioned manner, as in Lakedaimon.'

(In this passage ἀποφύγῃ is Keaney's emendation of ἀποφυγὴν and is no doubt right. But Keaney's translation of ἐνίων, 'in some states', seems wrong; Theophrastos is stating what ought to be done, and that must apply to all states. The point is rather that a second trial is usually before different judges; even if the court is the same one, the personnel changes in the course of time.)

In many legal systems, if a person is acquitted, he cannot be prosecuted again for the same offence. That was the rule in Athens, for example (Dem. 20.147, 24.54). But the passages just quoted show that in Sparta a fresh prosecution for the same offence was permitted. This is instanced by the fate of king Pausanias. On his return from his expedition to Athens in 403 he was accused of failure to exploit his military advantage over the Athenians, but was acquitted by majority vote (Paus. 3.5.2, quoted on page 141). Some years later, after the battle of Haliartos, he was put on trial on three charges, one of which was that 'having got the Athenian people at Peiraieus, he let them go', virtually the same as the charge on which he had already been acquitted (Xen. *Hell.* 3.5.25; cf. Bonner and Smith *CP* 37 (1942) 125). This time he was condemned to death in his absence.

PENALTIES

Whether the death penalty was required by law for any offence, or was imposed only when the judges considered it appropriate, is not known. But it was certainly used sometimes. There were two methods of execution. The first was to throw the condemned man into a pit called Kaiadas or Keadas.

> Paus. 4.18.4-5. τούτους ἔγνωσαν οἱ Λακεδαιμόνιοι ῥῖψαι πάντας ἐς τὸν Κεάδαν· ἐμβάλλουσι δὲ ἐνταῦθα οὓς ἂν ἐπὶ μεγίστοις τιμωρῶνται. οἱ μὲν δὴ ἄλλοι Μεσσηνίων ἐσπίπτοντες ἀπώλλυντο αὐτίκα, Ἀριστομένην δέ...
> 'The Lakedaimonians resolved to cast all these into Keadas; they throw in there whoever they punish for very serious offences. The rest of the Messenians, on falling in, perished immediately, but Aristomenes...'

Pausanias proceeds to relate Aristomenes's miraculous escape. His account makes clear that criminals were not executed before being thrown into the pit; normally they were killed by the fall. The pit is mentioned, with the name Kaiadas, by Thucydides: the ephors thought of casting into it the body of Pausanias the regent, who died of starvation

THE ADMINISTRATION OF JUSTICE

before trial (Thuc. 1.134.4). But Plutarch describes a quite different place and method used for execution in the third century.

> Plu. *Agis* 19.8. θάνατον αὐτοῦ κατεψηφίσαντο, καὶ τοὺς ὑπηρέτας ἐκέλευον ἄγειν εἰς τὴν καλουμένην Δεχάδα· τοῦτο δ' ἐστὶν οἴκημα τῆς εἱρκτῆς ἐν ᾧ θανατοῦσι τοὺς καταδίκους ἀποπνίγοντες. 'They condemned him (Agis IV) to death, and ordered the servants to take him into the so-called Dekhas; this is a room of the prison in which they put condemned persons to death by strangling.'

The sequel shows that 'strangling' here means hanging. First the grandmother of Agis and later his mother were admitted to the room; when his mother entered, 'she saw her son lying on the floor and her mother hanging dead from the noose' by which each had evidently been hanged in turn (Plu. *Agis* 20.4). The noose is mentioned also in the account of the same incident in the collection of apophthegms (Plu. *Eth.* 216d). When did the change from precipitation to hanging occur? A clue is provided by Herodotos in telling the legend of the Minyai and their wives.

> Hdt. 4.146.2-3. τοῖσι ὦν Λακεδαιμονίοισι ἔδοξε αὐτοὺς ἀποκτεῖναι, συλλαβόντες δέ σφεας κατέβαλον ἐς ἑρκτήν. κτείνουσι δὲ τοὺς ἂν κτείνωσι Λακεδαιμόνιοι νυκτός, μετ' ἡμέρην δὲ οὐδένα. ἐπεὶ ὦν ἔμελλόν σφεας καταχρήσεσθαι, παραιτήσαντο αἱ γυναῖκες τῶν Μινυέων, ἐοῦσαι ἀσταί τε καὶ τῶν πρώτων Σπαρτιητέων θυγατέρες, ἐσελθεῖν τε ἐς τὴν ἑρκτὴν καὶ ἐς λόγους ἐλθεῖν ἑκάστη τῷ ἑωυτῆς ἀνδρί. 'The Lakedaimonians resolved to execute them, and they arrested them and put them in prison. The Lakedaimonians execute at night whoever

they execute; they execute no one in daylight. When they were about to make away with them, the wives of the Minyai, who were of citizen birth, daughters of the foremost Spartiates, asked permission to enter the prison and speak with their respective husbands.'

There follows the tale of how the Minyai escaped from prison disguised in their wives' clothes. This is a legend, but it is clear that Herodotos is assuming for the legend the Spartan practices of his own time. We can accept it as a fact of the fifth century that executions were performed at night, the motive being perhaps a wish to conceal the shameful end of a Spartan. And Herodotos's account also implies that the executions were due to take place in the prison, from which the women did not expect to see their husbands emerge; there is nothing here about Kaiadas. So the best conclusion is that execution by hanging inside the prison, at night, was the normal practice by the fifth century. Perhaps Kaiadas was now used as a receptacle for the bodies after execution; alternatively the proposal to cast Pausanias the regent into it may have been an attempt to revive an obsolete practice to show abhorrence of an unusually wicked man.

It is remarkable that there is so little evidence for cases of homicide in Sparta that we cannot be sure what penalties were imposed for it. Xenophon does allude to one case, but even it is not quite clear.

> Xen. *An.* 4.8.25. ... Δρακόντιον Σπαρτιάτην, ὃς ἔφυγε παῖς ὢν οἴκοθεν, παῖδα ἄκων κατακανὼν ξυήλῃ πατάξας. '... Drakontios, a Spartiate, who went into exile from home when a boy, having unintentionally killed a boy by striking him with a whittle.'

At first sight this looks like a case of exile imposed as a penalty for unintentional homicide, and one is tempted to

THE ADMINISTRATION OF JUSTICE 147

jump to the conclusion that the rule of death for intentional homicide, exile for unintentional homicide, familiar to us from Athenian law, applied also in Sparta. That may be correct, but Xenophon's words do not prove it; for ἔφυγε could mean that Drakontios fled from Sparta to avoid trial and execution.

Certainly men expecting to be condemned to death did sometimes evade it by fleeing from Sparta before trial. King Pausanias fled to Tegea and lived for at least fifteen more years before he died there from an illness (Xen. *Hell.* 3.5.25, *IG* 5(1) 1565 (on p. xxi) = Tod *Greek Historical Inscriptions* no. 120). We hear nothing of any arrangements between Sparta and any other city for extradition of offenders. But a passage of Thucydides suggests that life outside Lakonia was not necessarily safe. It refers to king Pleistoanax, who was believed to have accepted a bribe from Perikles to withdraw the Spartan army from Attika in 446, and took refuge at Lykaion in Arkadia.

> Thuc. 5.16.3. φεύγοντα αὐτὸν ἐς Λύκαιον διὰ τὴν ἐκ τῆς Ἀττικῆς ποτε μετὰ δώρων δοκήσεως ἀναχώρησιν, καὶ ἥμισυ τῆς οἰκίας τοῦ ἱεροῦ τότε τοῦ Διὸς οἰκοῦντα φόβῳ τῷ Λακεδαιμονίων ... '... when he was in exile at Lykaion because of his withdrawal from Attika on one occasion with suspicion of bribery, and was living with half of his house within the precinct of Zeus at that time for fear of the Lakedaimonians ...'

This must mean that Pleistoanax wanted to be able to take sanctuary at a moment's notice if he saw any Spartans approaching, and it seems to imply that any Spartans who found him, even outside Lakonia, might either kill him on the spot or arrest him for execution in Sparta. Yet this is puzzling, because according to other evidence he had not been condemned to death. Ephoros and Plutarch say that he was condemned to a fine of 15 talents, and left Sparta because he was unable to pay it (Plu. *Per.* 22.3, schol. on Ar. *Clouds* 859 = *F. Gr. Hist.* 70 F193). Probably the explanation is that death was the penalty for failure to pay a fine.

Some other cases in which military commanders were condemned can be interpreted in the same way. Lysanoridas, one of the harmosts responsible for surrendering the Kadmeia to the Thebans, was condemned by the senate to pay a heavy fine, and left the Peloponnese (Plu. *Pelop.* 13.3, *Eth.* 598f); presumably he had not paid up, and thought that anywhere within the Peloponnese he might be caught and put to death. Thibron, after commanding in Asia, ζημιωθείς ἔφυγε (Xen. *Hell.* 3.1.8); that phrase seems to distinguish the formal penalty from the exile by using separate verbs for them, and so it probably means 'he was condemned to pay a fine and went into exile'. The case of Aristokles and Hipponoidas, two polemarchs who failed to obey an order from the king at the battle of Mantineia in 418, is more obscure; Thucydides says that they were found guilty of cowardice and went into exile (5.72.1), which could mean that exile was the formal penalty, but in view of the other cases I suspect that the formal penalty was a heavy fine and they went into exile to avoid execution for failure to pay it.

Other penalties for serious offences are exemplified in the inglorious career of king Leotykhidas. When accused of failure to restore to the people of Aigina some hostages taken from them, he was condemned to be sent to Aigina in place of the hostages (Hdt. 6.85.1), an interesting attempt to devise a special punishment to fit the crime. On that occasion, however, the penalty was in the end not carried out. Some years later he was found to have accepted bribes on an expedition to Thessaly; he went into exile (once again it is not

THE ADMINISTRATION OF JUSTICE

stated whether exile was the penalty or a means of avoiding the death penalty) and his house was demolished (Hdt. 6.72.2). Demolition of his house in this case will have been a way of demonstrating that the exile was to be permanent. But it was also possible for a man who was not exiled to have his house demolished as a penalty (Thuc. 5.63.2).

Besides death and exile, the other most serious penalty for a Spartan was disfranchisement; those were the three penalties which could be imposed only by the senate, not by the ephors (see page 127). Disfranchisement has been discussed on pages 42-6.

Kinadon and his fellow conspirators were whipped and goaded around the city (Xen. *Hell.* 3.3.11). (Presumably they were killed in the process or executed afterwards, though Xenophon does not say so explicitly.) They were not Spartan citizens, and there is no evidence that Spartiates were ever subjected to whipping (except boys: see page 55). But milder forms of ignominy could be imposed on Spartiates, such as the penalties for not marrying (see pages 75-6).

There is no reference to imprisonment as a penalty. The prison seems to have been used only to hold men awaiting trial or execution (e.g. Hdt. 4.146.2, Thuc. 1.131.2).

The commonest penalty was no doubt a monetary fine. Fines could be very large. The fine of 15 talents imposed on king Pleistoanax has already been mentioned. Phoibidas was fined the even larger sum of 100,000 drachmas, besides being dismissed from office, for occupying the Kadmeia in Thebes without authority (Plu. *Pelop.* 6.1); but in another passage Plutarch says that Agesilaos 'saved Phoibidas' (*Ages.* 23.11), which probably means that he got the fine cancelled, though we cannot tell by what procedure that was done (cf. de Ste. Croix *Origins* 135-6). Agis II was threatened with a fine of the same amount, besides demolition of his house, for his failure to subdue Argos, though in this case too in the end it was not imposed (Thuc. 5.63). It is hard to believe that any individuals in Sparta, even kings, had such large sums at their disposal. Perhaps these massive fines were nominal, and the real intention was to force the offenders into exile by imposing fines which they could not pay. But more often the ephors must have imposed small fines for all sorts of minor offences. Their complete freedom of action is strikingly illustrated by an occasion when they awarded an honour and a penalty at the same time for the same act. When the Thebans attacked Sparta in 362, Isadas, son of Phoibidas, entered the fray wearing neither armour nor clothes, and inflicted some harm on the enemy without being wounded himself.

> Plu. *Ages*. 34.11. ἐπὶ τούτῳ δὲ λέγεται τοὺς ἐφόρους στεφανώσαντας αὐτὸν εἶτα χιλίων δραχμῶν ἐπιβαλεῖν ζημίαν, ὅτι χωρὶς ὅπλων διακινδυνεύειν ἐτόλμησεν. 'For this act it is said that the ephors awarded him a crown, and then imposed a penalty of 1,000 drachmas for being so rash as to risk fighting without armour.'

Here the word ζημία is used of a fine, and it is sometimes assumed that this noun and its related verb ζημιόω, when used with the ephors as subject, always mean a monetary penalty. But the assumption is unsafe. These words are freely used of other kinds of penalty: examples in Spartan contexts include Xen. *LP* 10.5-7 (disfranchisement), Plu. *Lyk*. 17.6 (beating and starvation), *Lys*. 17.6 (death). So, although the ephors were not entitled to impose death or disfranchisement on their own authority, and a financial penalty was their most obvious weapon, we should use the translation 'punish' rather than 'fine' in other passages, leaving open the possibility that the ephors devised other kinds of punishment in some cases.

VIII

Conclusion

Our knowledge of Spartan law remains seriously incomplete. The foregoing chapters have assembled virtually all the evidence for the fifth and fourth centuries; yet there are great gaps. Even on some of the most obvious topics we are almost totally ignorant. For example, the Spartans must have had some rules, whether written or not, for assessing different varieties of homicide, distinguishing deliberate murder from accidental killing or pardonable self-defence; but what do we know of them? Only that killing of helots was legitimized by an annual declaration of war (see pages 36-7). The sole allusion to a particular case of homicide is ambivalent (see pages 146-7). Theft is another topic which one expects to find occupying a prominent place in any legal system. The Spartans certainly had a law of theft, for Xenophon alludes in passing to a law which prevents ἀποστερεῖν, wrongfully depriving someone of property (*Ages*. 4.2). But neither he nor any other author gives details, so that we know nothing whatever about the distinctions between types of theft and the penalties imposed for them.

The main reason for this incompleteness is that the only extensive texts devoted to Spartan law, Xenophon's *LP* and Plutarch's *Lykourgos*, both have the aim of explaining the ways in which the laws of Lykourgos differed from those of other cities, not the ways in which they were similar. To some extent this is true also of other authors, such as Herodotos and Aristotle, who mention particular Spartan laws more briefly. What they tell us is valuable, but it usually covers the unique or unusual features of the Spartan system. The modern reader is liable to get the impression that Sparta was a very strange place indeed, because his attention is seldom directed to the ways in which it was normal. As a working hypothesis, it would really be better to assume that Spartan law was much the same as Athenian law on all topics, such as homicide and theft, on which we are not told that it differed. But even this argument from silence cannot safely be applied to particular details.

In considering those features of Spartan law which were unique or unusual, Xenophon and Plutarch are surely right to single out military efficiency as the dominant purpose, and to emphasize especially the arrangements for the birth and upbringing of Spartiate boys. In Athens the family was a unit of great importance, whose autonomy was only gradually infringed by the state. In Sparta the state interfered much more. Marriage was controlled by law, to an extent which Athenians would have found intolerable, in order to maximize the production of good soldiers. It was not left to individuals and families to arrange marriages whenever they liked: there was a law against a woman's being married too young, and a law forbidding a man to marry late, badly, or not at all (see pages 72-6). When a woman was already married, she could, with her husband's consent, have intercourse with another man, so as to bear more children, even though this must sometimes have made it doubtful which man was the child's real father (see pages 83-8). When a boy was born, the parents were not free to rear him unless his health satisfied the inspecting elders (see pages 52-3). From the age of seven, the state took almost complete control of

CONCLUSION

the boys. An Athenian father was free to rear and educate his son in whatever way he thought fit, but a Spartan father had no such right.

> Plu. *Lyk.* 15.14. οὐκ ἰδίους ἡγεῖτο τῶν πατέρων τοὺς παῖδας, ἀλλὰ κοινοὺς τῆς πόλεως ὁ Λυκοῦργος, ὅθεν οὐκ ἐκ τῶν τυχόντων, ἀλλ' ἐκ τῶν ἀρίστων ἐβούλετο γεγονότας εἶναι τοὺς πολίτας. 'Lykourgos considered boys to be not the private property of their fathers but the common property of the city. Hence he wanted the citizens to be produced not from any chance parents but from the best.'

In the face of these facts it is surprising that a leading modern expert on the Greek family asserts that 'the family in the great period of Spartan power was always strong' (Lacey *Family* 207-8). The principal reason which Lacey gives is that, before the passing of the rhetra of Epitadeus, family succession was guaranteed. But in fact the family's rights of succession were not stronger in Sparta than in other cities, as far as is known; at some points they were weaker. The position before Epitadeus was that, if a man had a son, the son inherited his property; but that was equally true in Athens, where sons retained the right of automatic inheritance throughout the fourth century, after Spartan sons had lost it. If a man had no son, he might adopt one; but whereas in Athens a man could adopt whoever he wished, and only in rather exceptional cases chose someone who was not a relative (cf. Isaios 4.18), in Sparta it is likely that, before Epitadeus, his choice was restricted by a legal ban on the adoption of a man who already had a land lot (see pages 95-8). The right of the nearest relative to inherit, when there was no son and no adopted son, was presumably restricted by the same law against holding two lots, the purpose of which was to ensure that as many Spartiates as possible had leisure for soldiering. So even before Epitadeus the family's right of succession was weaker in Sparta than in Athens; after Epitadeus it was very weak indeed.

I conclude that the diminution of the rights and independence of the family is one of the most significant features of the Spartan legal system. It gave priority to the military requirements of the community. Such a system could hardly have been introduced, and could certainly not have continued in existence so long, without a general consensus of the heads of families that it should. The rhetra of Epitadeus, passed perhaps towards the end of the fifth century (see pages 104-5), is the earliest evidence we have that this consensus was beginning to break down. But what followed the breakdown was not a return to the primitive power of the family, but a move towards individuality. The rhetra of Epitadeus gave power to the individual to give or bequeath his property as he wished, without regard to the interests of the community. The licence given to individuals to acquire gold and silver money (whether the law forbidding this was repealed or merely ignored; see pages 119-20) was a further step in the same direction. Spartans began to live and act for themselves rather than for Sparta, and this was surely a major cause of Sparta's military downfall in the fourth century.

The other most significant feature is the administration of justice. Although a few major trials were in the hands of the kings and senators, it is clear that the great majority of judicial decisions were made by the five ephors alone, and many of them probably by only one or two ephors (see pages 129-32). Their power was amazingly tyrannical, as Plato observed (*Laws* 712d). They did not just enforce written laws, but imposed penalties for any conduct which they considered wrong.

> Plu. *Kleom.* 9.3 (Arist. fr. 539). προεκήρυττον οἱ ἔφοροι τοῖς πολίταις εἰς τὴν ἀρχὴν εἰσιόντες, ὡς Ἀριστοτέλης φησί, κείρεσθαι τὸν μύστακα καὶ προσέχειν τοῖς νόμοις, ἵνα μὴ χαλεποὶ ὦσιν αὐτοῖς, τὸ τοῦ μύστακος οἶμαι προτείνοντες, ὅπως καὶ περὶ τὰ μικρότατα τοὺς νέους πειθαρχεῖν ἐθίζωσι. 'On entering office the ephors used to proclaim to the citizens, as Aristotle says, "to cut their moustaches and observe the laws, or they would be hard on them". Their purpose in making the point about the moustache, I think, was to accustom young men to obedience in even the smallest matters.'

The form of words used in this proclamation implies that no law required the cutting of moustaches, but the ephors could order it on their own authority. If this proclamation was made every year, like a Roman praetor's *edictum perpetuum*, no doubt it became indistinguishable from a law; nevertheless it exemplifies the power of the ephors to impose rules. How could the Spartans tolerate this? It is not an adequate answer to compare the absolute power of kings in early times. A primitive people accepts the rulings of a monarch because any government is better than none, and also because the king is believed to have received from the gods a knowledge of what is right (Hom. *Il.* 2.205-6, 9.98-9, Hes. *Th.* 81-7). But the Spartans cannot have been influenced by those considerations; they could see that different legislative and judicial arrangements existed in other cities, and they did not think that the ephors enjoyed divine inspiration. Though elected, the ephors were just ordinary men (Arist. *Pol.* 1270b 28-31); Plato thought them similar to officials selected by lot (*Laws* 692a). The explanation can only be that the Spartans were quite confident that the notions of justice held by five, or even fewer, ordinary men would not differ significantly from those of the whole community. In Athens a jury of several hundred was needed to overcome the risk that citizens with idiosyncratic views might produce eccentric judgements. In Sparta there was, apparently, no such risk.

The conclusion to draw from this is that the Spartan legal system was established by a small and close-knit community of Spartiates among whom there was little or no dissent. The consensus prevailed until the late fifth century. Until then they accepted the laws about marriage, the *agoge*, and 'the life of honour', because they all agreed that the production of good soldiers should take priority over the interests and pleasures of the individual and the family. They accepted the ephors' judgements, not only because they were trained in youth to obey authority, but also because those were the judgements which any of them would have given. Thus Spartan law is not to be regarded as undemocratic, as far as the Spartiates themselves were concerned. To outsiders, including perioikoi and helots, it showed little consideration, but within the limits of citizenship it was a classic example of law embodying the popular will. No wonder, then, that the Spartiates' obedience to their law was famous in the time of Herodotos (7.104.4). But after that the consensus broke down, and many of the laws, instead of being amended and adapted to new opinions and new circumstances, began to be simply ignored: 'it is obvious that they obey neither God nor the laws of Lykourgos' (Xen. *LP* 14.7), 'but they secretly evade the law and enjoy the pleasures of the body' (Arist. *Pol.* 1270b 34-5). It is remarkable that the only substantial new laws which are known to have been made in the fifth and fourth centuries are the rhetra of Epitadeus and the law prohibiting individuals from holding gold and silver money, and the latter of these two soon ceased to be enforced. Instead of modernizing their law, the Spartans just ignored it; and that was why it failed in the end.

APPENDIX

The Age-Groups

The *agoge* comprised successive stages of training, and it is clear that, for part of it at least, different names were given to boys in each individual year. The definitions of these age-groups have been much discussed. A new piece of evidence was published by Diller *AJP* 62 (1941) 499-501; for subsequent discussion see Marrou *REA* 48 (1946) 216-30, Billheimer *TAPA* 77 (1946) 214-20, 78 (1947) 99-104, Chrimes *Sparta* 86-95, Michell *Sparta* 166-74, den Boer *Laconian Studies* 248-61, Tazelaar *Mn.* IV 20 (1967) 127-53, Brelich *Paides* 116-19, Toynbee *Problems* 318, Hodkinson *Chiron* 13 (1983) 241-2.

Plutarch mentions specific ages at four points in his account.

> Plu. *Lyk.* 16.7. πάντας εὐθὺς ἑπταετεῖς γενομένους παραλαμβάνων αὐτὸς εἰς ἀγέλας κατελόχιζε. 'As soon as they were seven years old he (Lykourgos) took them all over himself and brigaded them in companies.'

> Plu. *Lyk.* 16.12. γενόμενοι δὲ δωδεκαετεῖς ἄνευ χιτῶνος ἤδη διετέλουν ... 'When they were twelve years old, they now lived without a tunic ...'

> Plu. *Lyk.* 17.3-4. εἴρενας δὲ καλοῦσι τοὺς ἔτος ἤδη δεύτερον ἐκ παίδων γεγονότας, μελλείρενας δὲ τῶν παίδων τοὺς πρεσβυτάτους. οὗτος οὖν ὁ εἴρην εἴκοσιν ἔτη γεγονὼς ἄρχει τε τῶν ὑποτεταγμένων ... '"Eiren" is the

name given to those now in the second year of age after boyhood, and "melleiren" to the oldest of the boys. So this eiren, being twenty years old, commands those set under him...'

Plu. *Lyk.* 25.1. οἱ μέν γε νεώτεροι τριάκοντ' ἐτῶν τὸ παράπαν οὐ κατέβαινον εἰς ἀγοράν, ἀλλὰ διὰ τῶν συγγενῶν καὶ τῶν ἐραστῶν ἐποιοῦντο τὰς ἀναγκαίας οἰκονομίας. 'Those younger than thirty years used not to go down into the Agora at all, but they made their necessary purchases through their relatives and their lovers.'

Some scholars (especially Tazelaar) have worried over the exact meaning of the expressions specifying ages: does ἑπταετεῖς γενομένους, for instance, mean that each boy was recruited on his seventh birthday, or at the age of seven (between his seventh and eighth birthdays), or in his seventh year (between his sixth and seventh birthdays)? This worry is misplaced, because it is most unlikely that the Spartans themselves were meticulous about each boy's age. They had no birth certificates, and their calendar did not make it easy to calculate ages. Even in Athens, a far more literate society, a fourth-century speech shows that there was no way of proving which of two half-brothers was the elder (Dem. 39.27-9); and when young men were registered in their demes, there was sometimes no way of checking whether they were eighteen years old except by inspecting their physical development (Ar. *Wasps* 578). So the Spartans probably on one particular day each year (perhaps the first day of the year) just recruited all the boys who looked as if they were aged about seven; those boys would then proceed together through the *agoge* year by year, becoming eirens when they were about twenty.

APPENDIX — THE AGE-GROUPS

More detailed information is given in two glosses on the words 'eiren' and 'melleiren', attached to Herodotos and Strabo respectively. (Here I omit the sentences containing comments on the accentuation of words in -ην.)

Λέξεις Ἡροδότου (H. Stein's *editio maior* of Hdt., vol. 2 p. 465; reprinted in Latte's *Lexica Graeca Minora*, p. 213). εἰρήν· παρὰ Λακεδαιμονίοις ἐν τῷ πρώτῳ ἐνιαυτῷ ὁ παῖς ῥωβίδας καλεῖται, τῷ δευτέρῳ προκομιζόμενος, τῷ τρίτῳ μικιζόμενος, τῷ τετάρτῳ πρόπαις, τῷ πέμπτῳ παῖς, τῷ ἕκτῳ μελείρην. ἐφηβεύει δὲ παρ' αὐτοῖς ὁ παῖς ἀπὸ ἐτῶν δεκατεσσάρων μέχρι καὶ εἴκοσιν. (The word μελείρην should be emended to μελλείρην.) '*Eiren*: among the Lakedaimonians, in the first year the boy is called "rhobidas", in the second "prokomizomenos", in the third "mikizomenos", in the fourth "propais", in the fifth "pais", in the sixth "melleiren". Among them the boy is an ephebe from fourteen years right up to twenty.'

Paris 1397 fol. 225v-226r (published by Diller *AJP* 62 (1941) 500). μελλείρην, παρὰ Λακεδαιμονίοις ὁ μέλλων εἰρὴν ἔσεσθαι. ἐφηβεύει μὲν γὰρ παρὰ Λακεδαιμονίοις ὁ παῖς ἐπ' ἐτῶν ιδ´ μέχρι κ´. καλεῖται δὲ τῷ μὲν πρώτῳ ἐνιαυτῷ ῥωβίδας, τῷ δὲ δευτέρῳ προκομιζόμενος, τῷ τρίτῳ μικιζόμενος, τῷ δ´ πρόπαις, τῷ ε´ παῖς, τῷ ϛ´ μελλείρην, τῷ ζ´ εἰρήν. (ἐπ' should be emended to ἀπ'.) '*Melleiren*: among the Lakedaimonians, one who is about to be an eiren. Among the Lakedaimonians the boy is an ephebe from fourteen years to twenty. He is called in the first year "rhobidas", in the second "prokomizomenos", in the third "mikizomenos", in the fourth "propais", in the fifth "pais", in the sixth "melleiren", in the seventh "eiren".'

These are clearly two versions of the same gloss. The first version lists the six year-names before giving the age of an ephebe; and when only this version was known, some scholars took the six year-names to refer either to the first six years of a boy's life or to the first six years after he entered the *agoge*. But the second version, not known until Diller's publication in 1941, gives the age of an ephebe first and means that the year-names refer to that period; thus a rhobidas was fourteen, a prokomizomenos fifteen, a mikizomenos sixteen, a propais seventeen, a pais eighteen, a melleiren nineteen, and an eiren twenty. This interpretation is preferable, because it agrees with Plutarch's statement that an eiren was twenty. It is in fact quite easy even in the first version of the gloss to take the sentence giving the age of an ephebe to refer to the same period as the year-names. Those (Marrou, Billheimer) who maintain the alternative interpretation, that a rhobidas was seven and so on, have to say that 'this eiren' in Plutarch means an eiren put in charge of a company and does not imply that all eirens were as old as twenty. That, though not impossible, is awkward; it is much easier to take 'twenty years old' as a clarifying synonym of the phrase ἔτος ἤδη δεύτερον ἐκ παίδων γεγονότας. But that too is an odd phrase. There seems to be no parallel for this form of expression (γεγονώς with ἔτος and an ordinal numeral, instead of a cardinal, in the accusative). We must therefore be cautious in interpreting it. Does it mean that the eirens had reached or completed the second year after boyhood, so that there was an interval of one or two years between ceasing to be a melleiren (the oldest of the boys) and becoming an eiren? Tazelaar takes that view (and builds on it an incredible theory that the Spartans used simultaneously two different systems of classifying boys by age, one 'legal' and one 'physical'), but it is contradicted by the second version of the gloss, in which

APPENDIX — THE AGE-GROUPS

the melleiren and the eiren are in consecutive years. We should therefore follow those (Chrimes, den Boer) who interpret δεύτερον as 'next' (cf. LSJ δεύτερος I.2); when a youth ceased to be a boy, he was an eiren for the next year.

The same sentence of Plutarch shows that boyhood was regarded as ending at the age of twenty, but the ambiguity of παῖς, 'boy', should be noticed. Besides its general meaning, it was also the specific name for those in one particular year, the age of eighteen. With these year-names one may compare British and American university expressions like 'freshman' and 'sophomore'; and anyone disposed to criticize the Spartans for using 'boy' for an age-group near the senior end of the list may pause to reflect that in America 'junior' is a general word for a boy or youth and is also the specific name for an undergraduate in the penultimate year of his course. Such terms are conventional rather than descriptive. It therefore does not matter that the origins of the terms 'rhobidas', 'prokomizomenos', and 'mikizomenos' are uncertain; even if their origins were known, that would not tell us anything about how the words were used in practice, and in this connection arguments from etymology, such as those offered by Marrou and Billheimer, are rightly rejected by den Boer.

'Mikizomenos' may indeed be a false form. Inscriptions of the Roman period (IG 5(1) 256, 276, 286, 292, etc.) give a word μικιχιζόμενος (with some variations such as μικκιχιδδόμενος). That might possibly be a different word, but it is much more likely that it is the same word and there is textual corruption in both versions of the gloss; for not only would the textual corruption by haplography be very easy, but also in one of the inscriptions (IG 5(1) 287) the person who is named as a mikikhizomenos is said to be a συνέφηβος of someone else, which implies that he is within the ephebic age-range. So it is best to take 'mikikhizomenos' as the correct word for a youth of sixteen. Inscriptions also give the words πρατοπάμπαις (*IG* 5(1) 256, 270, 273, 279, etc.) and ἀτροπάμπαις (*IG* 5(1) 278, 279), but without indicating the ages to which they refer.

So the landmarks in a boy's life seem to have been these: at seven he left home and entered the *agoge* (Plu. *Lyk*. 16.7); at twelve his life became more austere, with less clothing and no baths (Plu. *Lyk*. 16.12); at fourteen he became an ephebe (glosses on Herodotos and Strabo); at twenty he ceased to be a boy and became an eiren (Plu. *Lyk*. 17.3-4, glosses on Herodotos and Strabo). The significance of being an ephebe is not explained, but probably it means that military training began at fourteen. Whether an eiren was still regarded as an ephebe is not quite clear; that may seem to be implied by the phrase 'in the seventh "eiren"' in the gloss on Strabo, but it is probably better to take it as meaning that a young man was an eiren after completing six years as an ephebe, not that he was still an ephebe in that year.

Plu. *Lyk*. 25.1 shows that the age of thirty was another turning-point in the life of a Spartiate, but it is difficult to determine whether he was an eiren for the whole period from twenty to thirty or only for the first year. Plu. *Lyk*. 17.3-4 and the gloss on Strabo can be taken as meaning that it was only for one year, at the age of twenty. But alternatively it is possible to take both those texts as meaning that that was the first of the years in which a young man was an eiren, so that twenty was the minimum, rather than the only, age for that grade; and this interpretation is supported by several other considerations. First, Xen. *LP* 2.11 and Plu. *Lyk*. 17.2 agree in saying that only the best of the eirens were selected to take charge of the companies of boys. We do not know how many boys there were in a company, but it is hard to think that one

APPENDIX — THE AGE-GROUPS 165

eiren would have sole charge of more than about a dozen. With thirteen year-groups of boys (from seven to nineteen), the single year-group of twenty-year-olds would not have been large enough to offer a choice of leaders. Secondly, there is some further evidence of vocabulary. The lexicon of Photios (ed. Naber, under κατὰ πρωτείρας) defines πρωτεῖραι as οἱ περὶ εἴκοσιν ἔτη παρὰ Λάκωσι, 'those about twenty years old among the Lakonians' (cf. Hesykhios κ 1358); and an inscription from Thouria (not from Sparta itself, but Thouria was controlled by Sparta) mentions τριτίρενες (*IG* 5(1) 1386). Perhaps a man was an εἴρην from twenty to thirty, and in the first year of that period was called πρωτείρης (or, if we emend Photios, πρωτείρην), in the third year τριτείρην, and so on. This suggestion (first made by Foucart) fits in with a widely accepted interpretation of Hdt. 9.85.1-2, where the readings ἱρέας and ἱρέες are generally emended to ἰρένας and ἰρένες (assumed to be an Ionic or Doric form of εἴρ-), so that Herodotos says that after the battle of Plataia the Spartans made three tombs for their dead, one for the eirens, one for the other Spartiates, and one for the helots. If the eirens were all the Spartiates below the age of thirty, that gives a reasonably equal distribution of numbers among the three tombs. But the emendations (first suggested by Valckenaer) are rejected by den Boer *Laconian Studies* 288-98; he prefers to keep the manuscripts' readings and argues that a special tomb was provided for priests. There is indeed one serious difficulty with the emendations: those buried in this tomb included four named men who had been especially distinguished in the battle, one of whom commanded a *lokhos* (Amompharetos, Hdt. 9.53.2), but could he have been under thirty? Perhaps that is not impossible. In wartime rapid promotion sometimes occurs, and many good Spartiates had recently died at Thermopylai. It may be that at Plataia a *lokhos* was commanded by an outstanding man under thirty, even though in another context Xenophon can regard an eiren as not an ἀνήρ (*LP* 2.11). So, in view of the evidence for the existence of words like πρωτείρην and τριτείρην (which den Boer does not consider), I am inclined to accept hesitantly that a Spartiate remained an eiren up to the age of thirty.

Xenophon in *LP* employs some different terminology to refer to the stages of upbringing of boys. After discussing the birth of children in chapter 1, he proceeds to παῖδες in chapter 2. Chapter 3 begins ὅταν γε μὴν ἐκ παίδων εἰς τὸ μειρακιοῦσθαι ἐκβαίνωσι, 'when they pass out of boyhood into adolescence'. One might expect those passing out of boyhood to become men, and μειρακιοῦσθαι is a verb which does not occur elsewhere in the classical period: should we follow Cobet in deleting εἰς τὸ μειρακιοῦσθαι as a late gloss? No, because the chapter ends καὶ τῶν μὲν αὖ παιδίσκων οὕτως ἐπεμελήθη, 'and that was how he attended to the young laddies'. Adults could hardly be called παιδίσκοι; so this chapter is about teenagers, who can be either distinguished from boys or treated as a subdivision of boys, and Xenophon's reason for inserting the phrase εἰς τὸ μειρακιοῦσθαι is precisely to make clear that on this occasion ἐκ παίδων does not mean arrival at adulthood. (For παιδίσκος used of an age older than παῖς but younger than ἡβῶν, cf. Xen. *Hell.* 5.4.32.) Chapter 4 proceeds to ἡβῶντες: these are ἄνδρες, 'men' (4.3). In 4.7 Xenophon comes to 'those who have passed through the age of ἥβη, out of whom appointments are made to the greatest offices'. The best explanation of this is that chapter 3 is about ephebes between the ages of fourteen and twenty, and in chapter 4 the ἡβῶντες are the young men between twenty and thirty. (A ἡβῶν is not necessarily as young as an ἔφηβος. The word is vague, but in Ar. *Wasps* 357, for example, it is used of a man old enough to

APPENDIX — THE AGE-GROUPS

be on military service overseas.) Taking the age of thirty from Plu. *Lyk.* 25.1, which says that men below that age did not go to the Agora (and Plu. *Agis* 12.4 shows that the ephors' official seats were in the Agora), we can interpret *LP* 4.7 as meaning that it was only at the age of thirty that a man became eligible to be an ephor or to hold other important offices. There is only one difficulty about this interpretation. Xenophon says that permission to grow the hair long was given τοῖς ὑπὲρ τὴν ἡβητικὴν ἡλικίαν, 'to those over the age of ἥβη' (*LP* 11.3). That phrase is so similar to τοῖς τὴν ἡβητικὴν ἡλικίαν πεπερακόσιν (*LP* 4.7), which I have argued means the age of thirty, that one might expect it to have the same meaning. Yet Plutarch says that long hair was allowed εὐθὺς ἐκ τῆς τῶν ἐφήβων ἡλικίας, 'immediately after the age of the ephebes' (*Lyk.* 22.2), which must mean at twenty. The preferable solution is to distinguish between ὑπέρ and πεπερακώς. What Xenophon calls ἡ ἡβητικὴ ἡλικία is the period of ten years between the ages of twenty and thirty; ὑπέρ means 'having attained' this period, at twenty, while πεπερακώς means 'having passed' it, at thirty.

Spartans performed military service from the age of twenty, and the expression τὰ δέκα ἀφ' ἥβης (Xen. *Hell.* 2.4.32, 3.4.23, 4.5.14, *Ages.* 1.31) means the part of the army between the ages of twenty and thirty (cf. Billheimer *TAPA* 77 (1946) 214-20). This looks like official usage. As a term of Spartan law, probably ἥβη meant a particular point of time, the moment at which a youth ceased to be a boy and became a man, at the age of twenty. The use of the words ἡβῶντες and ἡ ἡβητικὴ ἡλικία for men who have reached the age of ἥβη but have not yet reached the next landmark, the age of thirty, may be just popular usage (rather as in English we continue saying that a person 'is twenty' as long as he has not yet reached the age of twenty-one).

Index of Passages

Aelian
  Var. Hist. 3.10: 63-5
  — 6.1: 33
  — 6.6: 76, 121
  — 12.43: 47-50
Alkman (ed. Page)
  98: 111
Andokides
  1.95-6: 3
  1.126-7: 54
Antiphanes
  44.3: 111
Aristophanes
  Birds 1012-13: 115
  — 1281-2: 15
  Lys. 78-84: 72
  Wasps 357: 166
  — 527: 69
  — 578: 160
  schol. on *Clouds* 859: 148
  schol. on *Knights* 634: 48
  schol. on *Wealth* 279: 48
Aristotle
  Politics 1263a 35-7: 114
  — 1265b 37-8: 127
  — 1269a 29-1271b 19: 16
  — 1269b 19-23: 72, 87, 104
  — 1270a 6-8: 72, 103, 104
  — 1270a 15-34: 92, 101-10
  — 1270a 23-5: 81, 96
  — 1270a 27: 96
  — 1270a 29-30: 98
  — 1270a 34-6: 51, 98
  — 1270b 1-4: 76, 103-4
  — 1270b 5-6: 95, 110
  — 1270b 11-13: 16
  — 1270b 24-5: 26, 127
  — 1270b 28-31: 129-30, 155
  — 1270b 34-5: 156
  — 1271a 5-6: 127, 131
  — 1271a 9-18: 126
  — 1271a 26-37: 43, 111-12
  — 1271b 13-15: 28
  — 1271b 24-30: 103
  — 1272a 13-15: 112
  — 1275b 7-12: 135
  — 1275b 9-10: 127, 130
  — 1285a 6-7: 124
  — 1285a 7-10: 70, 125-6
  — 1294b 33-4: 127
  — 1306a 18-19: 126
  — 1306b 36-1307a 2: 92
  — 1333b 11-21: 16
  fr. 532-45: 17
  — 533: 2
  — 538: 36-7
  — 539: 21, 155
  — 543: 115
Athenaios
  141a-c: 112

141f: 27
271e-f: 39, 47
555b-c: 79-80
657d: 32, 36
Demosthenes
 18.210: 131
 20.147: 143
 24.54: 143
 39.27-9: 160
 41.3: 87
 44.10: 82
 57.20: 82
 57.43: 87
Diodoros
 11.50: 7
 12.65.9: 29
 19.70.5: 44
Diogenes Laertios
 2.51-2: 8
 2.54: 49
Ephoros (*F. Gr. Hist.* 70)
 F117: 23-5, 28, 34
 F193: 148
Harpokration
 τριακάς: 120
Hellanikos (*F. Gr. Hist.* 4)
 F116: 2
Herakleides Lembos
 Exc. Pol. 12: 93, 106
 — 13: 114
[Herakleitos]
 Epist. 9.2: 50
Hermippos of Smyrna
 Περὶ νομοθετῶν: 79-80
Herodotos
 1.65: 1-3, 14

1.66.1: 2
3.148.2: 131
4.145.5: 50-1
4.146.2-3: 145-6, 149
5.39.1: 82
5.40: 83
5.49-51: 140
5.68.2: 26
5.75.2: 123
6.57.4-5: 77, 96, 107, 123, 127
6.58: 122
6.60: 118
6.61-7: 86
6.63: 82, 132
6.65.2: 77-8
6.66.1: 134
6.71.2: 77
6.72.2: 149
6.82: 131, 137, 140-1
6.85.1: 133, 148
7.3.3: 126
7.104.4-5: 14, 156
7.134: 93, 118
7.204: 2
7.231: 44
7.234.2: 27, 99
7.239.4: 82
8.124.3: 67
9.10.1: 35
9.11.3: 28
9.35.1: 50-1
9.53.2: 165
9.81: 119
9.85.1-2: 165
gloss on εἰρήν: 161-4

Hesiod
 Theogony 81-7: 155
Hesykhios
 α 3769: 58
 β 865-7: 54
 ε 5042: 96
 κ 1358: 165
 μ 1538: 49
 μ 1544: 48
 ν 314: 40
Homer
 Iliad 2.205-6: 155
 — 9.98-9: 155
Hypereides
 Ath. 29: 116
Inscriptiones Graecae 5(1)
 18b: 133
 32b: 133
 60.4: 48
 71a.7: 48
 128.13: 111
 150.1: 111
 155.6: 111
 256-92: 163-4
 480: 26
 564-6: 26
 680: 26
 688: 26
 701-14: 121
 937: 30
 1228-32: 38
 1386: 165
 1507.1: 111
 1565: 147
Isaios
 3.45-51: 108

 4.18: 153
 6.12-13: 139
Isokrates
 4.111: 49
 12.66: 37
 12.177-81: 27-8
 12.181: 30, 127, 137
 12.211-12: 58, 60-1
Kritias (Diels-Kranz 88)
 B32-7: 15
Law of Gortyn
 12.17-19: 73
Lykourgos
 Leokrates 107: 69-70
 — 129: 5, 70
Lysias
 1.14: 120
 30.11: 128
 32.4: 82
Menander
 Aspis 85: 108
 — 279-81: 108
 Dyskolos 729-39: 108
Myron (*F. Gr. Hist.* 106)
 F1: 39-40
 F2: 32, 36
Pausanias
 2.9.1: 133
 3.5.2: 128, 141, 144
 3.6.2: 135
 3.14.2: 53
 3.15.8: 53
 3.16.9: 26
 3.20.6: 35
 4.14.4-5: 33
 4.18.1-3: 92-3

INDEX OF PASSAGES

4.18.4-5: 144
Philo
  Special Laws 3.22: 82
Photios
  Lex. κατὰ πρωτείρας: 165
Phylarkhos (*F. Gr. Hist.* 81)
  F43: 47-50
Pindar
  schol. on *Ol*. 6.154: 29
Plato
  Alk. 122d: 38
  — 122e: 119
  Apol. 37a: 142
  Laws 629a: 51
  — 633c: 75
  — 637a: 114
  — 684d-685a: 89
  — 692a: 155
  — 712d: 154
  — 923c-926d: 95
  Phdr. 260c: 22
  Prot. 342c: 115
  Rep. 457d: 86
  — 544c: 16
  Symp. 210c: 64
  schol. on *Laws* 630e: 96
Plutarch
  Ages. 1.2: 54
  — 1.4: 43, 48, 54
  — 7.6-7: 124-5
  — 19.10: 19
  — 20.2: 49
  — 23.11: 149
  — 24.3: 68
  — 24.9-26.1: 141
  — 30.2-6: 44-5
  — 32.11: 132
  — 34.11: 150
  Agis 3.1: 119
  — 4.1: 109
  — 4.2: 19, 48
  — 5: 100-10
  — 5.1: 119
  — 5.2: 94-5
  — 5.3-4: 3, 5-6
  — 5.5: 42
  — 5.7: 51
  — 6.7: 109
  — 7.1-7: 109
  — 8-11: 5
  — 8: 99
  — 8.1: 3, 6-7, 91
  — 9-10: 7
  — 9.1: 5
  — 9.3: 20
  — 9.6: 109
  — 11.1: 7
  — 11.2: 116
  — 12.4: 132, 167
  — 13.2: 107
  — 13.3: 106
  — 19.5-8: 141
  — 19.8: 145
  — 19.10: 135
  — 20.4: 145
  Arat. 38.12: 19-21
  Comp. Lyk. Num. 2.7: 38
  Ethika 208d: 22
  — 210a: 22, 55
  — 212b: 55
  — 216d: 145
  — 217a-b: 142

Plutarch, *Ethika (contd.)*
— 218d: 136
— 221a-b: 131, 135
— 221f: 128
— 226f-227a: 133
— 227b: 3
— 227f: 81
— 233b: 22
— 233f: 58
— 238c: 93
— 238d: 115
— 239d-e: 32-4
— 598f: 148
Kleom. 1.1: 73
— 1.2: 109
— 5.3-4: 20
— 8.1: 48
— 9.3: 21, 155
— 10: 19
— 10.1: 132
— 23.1: 34
— 28.2: 20
— 30.3: 20
Lyk. 1: 2, 17, 18
— 5.6: 1
— 6: 3-4, 18-19, 26-7
— 8.1: 90
— 8.5-7: 25, 28, 33, 90-9, 105
— 9.1-2: 118
— 12: 111-13
— 12.5: 133
— 13.1: 3
— 13.5-7: 114
— 13.11: 3
— 14.3-7: 71-2
— 15.1-3: 75
— 15.4-9: 66, 73, 78-9, 113
— 15.12-14: 74, 84-7, 153
— 15.16-18: 87
— 16.1-2: 27, 52-4, 71, 94-5
— 16.7: 159-64
— 16.8: 56
— 16.12: 159-64
— 17.1: 61
— 17.2-4: 26, 54-6, 66, 159-64
— 17.5-6: 58, 60-1, 150
— 18.2: 19
— 18.5-8: 57-8, 61-5
— 21.4-6: 18-19
— 22.1: 54
— 22.2: 66, 167
— 24.2: 32, 43, 117
— 25.1: 61, 66, 160-7
— 25.2-3: 53
— 25.6: 67
— 26.1-5: 126-7
— 27.1-4: 120-2
— 27.6-7: 115-16
— 28.7: 36-7
— 29.10-11: 5
— 30.1: 119
— 31.7: 18
Lys. 2.1-2: 49
— 17.2-6: 5-6, 118-19, 150
— 19.7: 119, 128
— 30.1: 140
— 30.7: 73-4
Pelop. 6.1: 149
— 13.3: 148

INDEX OF PASSAGES

Per. 22.3-4: 44, 49, 148
Phok. 20.4: 49
Pyrrh. 26.21: 49
Them. 32.2: 82
— 32.4: 20
Polyainos
  Strat. 2.21: 140
Polybios
  2.56: 20
  5.19.2-3: 26
  6.45.3: 89-92
  12.6b.8: 85
Polydeukes
  3.83: 40
Souda
  ε 2384: 96
  μ 1188: 48
  σ 630: 48
Stephanos of Byzantion
  Δυμᾶνες: 26
Stobaios
  3.40.8: 50
Strabo:
  8.5.4: 23-5, 35
  8.5.5: 2
  10.4.18: 67
  gloss on μελλείρην: 161-4
Teles
  Περὶ φυγῆς: 50
Theophrastos
  Laws: 138-43
Thucydides
  1.10.2: 26
  1.18.1: 2, 15
  1.101.2: 31, 38
  1.103.1: 38

1.131.2: 137, 149
1.133: 137
1.134.4: 145
1.144.2: 115
2.25.2: 29
2.39.1: 115
3.52.3: 133
4.8.9: 105
4.53.2: 29-30
4.55.2: 67
4.57.3: 29
4.80.3: 35
5.16.3: 147
5.26.5: 14
5.34.1: 35, 41-2
5.34.2: 44-6
5.54.1: 27, 28
5.63: 134, 149-50
5.67.1: 41
5.72.1: 148
5.72.4: 67
7.19.3: 35, 40
8.5.1: 40
8.5.2: 11
8.22.1: 28
Tyrtaios (ed. West)
  1: 92
  4: 4
  6-7: 33-4
  19.8: 26
Xenophon
  Ages. 1.31: 167
  — 4.2: 151
  — 5.2: 22
  — 9.6: 109
  — 11.4: 22

Xenophon (*contd.*)
  An. 4.6.14: 59
  — 4.8.25: 146-7
  — 6.6.28: 3
  Hell. 1.2.18: 29
  — 2.4.29: 76, 132
  — 2.4.32: 167
  — 2.4.36: 132
  — 3.1.4: 29, 40
  — 3.1.8: 148
  — 3.3.1-4: 86, 122, 134-5, 140
  — 3.3.4-11: 131, 137
  — 3.3.5-6: 40, 42, 46, 117
  — 3.3.8: 31
  — 3.3.10: 29
  — 3.3.11: 127-8, 149
  — 3.4.8: 124
  — 3.4.23: 167
  — 3.5.25: 144, 147
  — 4.5.14: 167
  — 5.2.35: 133
  — 5.3.9: 42, 46-9
  — 5.4.13: 68
  — 5.4.24: 141
  — 5.4.32: 166
  — 6.4.10: 67
  — 6.5.21: 28
  — 6.5.28: 35
  — 7.1.12: 35
  — 7.1.25: 29
  LP 1.1: 9
  — 1.3-4: 15, 37, 71-2
  — 1.6-9: 72-4, 83-7, 95
  — 2.2: 55
  — 2.5: 56
  — 2.6-8: 59
  — 2.10: 56-7
  — 2.11: 54, 56, 66, 164, 166
  — 2.13-14: 61-5
  — 3.1: 166
  — 3.3: 42-3, 52, 58, 64
  — 3.5: 9, 166
  — 4.3-7: 9, 66-7, 166-7
  — 5.2: 111
  — 5.7-8: 68-9, 114
  — 6.1-2: 57
  — 6.2-3: 9
  — 6.3: 85, 114
  — 6.5: 9
  — 7.2: 43, 117
  — 7.5: 118
  — 7.6: 9, 14, 119
  — 8.4: 129, 131, 137
  — 8.5: 3
  — 9.4-6: 14, 44-5, 74, 77
  — 10.1-3: 127
  — 10.5-7: 150
  — 10.7: 25, 43, 52, 58, 69, 112
  — 10.8: 2
  — 11.1: 10
  — 11.2: 67
  — 11.3: 66, 121, 167
  — 12.5: 68-9
  — 13.1: 25
  — 13.5: 14, 132
  — 13.7: 118
  — 13.11: 76, 124-5, 132
  — 14: 8-14

— 14.3: 119
— 14.4: 115-16
— 14.7: 156
— 15: 10

— 15.3: 27-8
— 15.6: 132
— 15.9: 122
Oik. 7.5: 73

Index of Greek Words

ἀγάμιον: 74
ἀγέλα: 54
ἀγωγή: 42-3, 46-51, 54-68, 159-64
ἀδέσποτοι: 39
αἰδώς: 55
ἀκμάζειν: 67
ἁλίσκεσθαι: 61
ἄμπαιδες: 58
ἀνακρίνειν, ἀνάκρισις: 139
ἀνδρεῖον: 111
ἀποπέμπειν: 82
ἀποστερεῖν: 151
ἁρμόζειν: 11, 80
ἁρπαγή, ἁρπάζειν: 78-80
ἄρχειν: 55, 57
ἀτιμία: 44
ἀτροπάμπαις: 164
ἀφέται: 39
ἄφρουρος: 76

βοῦα: 54

γέροντες: 123
γράφειν: 5
γυμνάσιον: 69

δέκα ἀφ᾽ ἥβης: 66, 167
δεσποσιοναῦται: 39

δεύτερος: 162-3
δοῦλος: 25, 37-8

ἐγγύη: 77, 80
εἴρην: 54-8, 66-8, 160-6
ἐκεῖ: 14
ἑλλανοδίκης: 124-5
ἐπίκληρος: 96, 107-8
ἐπιπαματίς, ἐπιπταματίς: 96
ἐρυκτῆρες: 39
ἔφηβος: 161-7

ζημία, ζημιοῦν: 148, 150

ἥβη, ἡβῶν: 66, 166-7

ἴλα: 54
ἱππαγρέται: 66-7
ἱππεῖς: 67

κακογάμιον: 74
καλά: 42
καλοὶ κἀγαθοί: 26
κάσεν: 48
κατὰ ἔτος: 30
κήδεσθαι: 64-5
κλάριον: 106-7
κληρονόμος: 107-8

INDEX OF GREEK WORDS

κρυπτεία: 37
κυθηροδίκης: 29-30

Λακεδαιμόνιοι: 25, 35
λέσχη: 52-3

μάγειρος: 118
μαστιγοφόροι: 55
μειρακιοῦσθαι: 166
μελλείρην: 160-3
μήν: 12
μικιζόμενος, μικιχιζόμενος: 161-4
μόθαξ: 46-51
μόθων: 48
μοιχεία: 87

νεοδαμώδης: 39-41, 51, 117
νόμιμα: 43, 52
νομοθέτης: 103-4, 106
νόμος: 1-3, 106
νομοφύλαξ: 133
νῦν: 12

ξενηλασία: 115

ὅμοιος: 25, 42
ὀψιγάμιον: 74

παιδίσκος: 166
παῖς: 161-3, 166
πάλιν: 11-12
πατρονόμος: 133
πατρωιοῦχος: 96
πειθώ: 55

ποιεῖσθαι: 87-8
πόλις: 27
πολιτικὴ χώρα: 91
πρατοπάμπαις: 164
προβουλεύειν: 7
προκομιζόμενος: 161-3
πρόπαις: 161-2
πρωτείρην, πρωτείρης: 165-6

ῥήτρα: 3-5
ῥωβίδας: 161-3

σκυτάλη: 139
Σπαρτιάτης: 25, 42
συμβόλαιον: 130
συμβολεύειν: 56
συντελεῖν: 25, 28, 91
σύντροφος: 48
συσκήνιον: 111
συσσίτιον: 111

τεκνοποιεῖσθαι: 87
τετταράκοντα ἀφ' ἥβης: 68
τρέσαντες: 44
τριτείρην: 165-6
τρόφιμος: 47-8

ὑπομείονες: 46

φειδείτιον, φιδίτιον: 111
φεύγειν: 147-8
φυλή: 26-7, 52-4

ὠβά: 26-7

Index of Subjects

absence of defendant from trial: 141
adoption: 86-8, 95-8, 153-4
adultery: 87
age-groups: 159-67
Agesikles (king): 2
Agesilaos II: 8, 13-14, 17, 21-2, 44, 49, 109, 124-5, 132, 140, 149
Agesipolis I: 47
Agis I: 24
Agis II: 133-4, 141, 149
Agis IV: 5-7, 17, 19-20, 91, 99, 109, 135, 141, 145
agoge: 42-3, 46-51, 54-68, 159-64
Agora, avoided by young men: 167
aliens, disputes with Spartans: 125, 132-3
    expelled from Sparta: 115, 131
Amompharetos: 165
Anaxandridas II: 82-3, 86, 142-3
apophthegms: 21-2
Apothetai: 53
arbitration: 136
Areus I: 135
Aristokles: 148

Aristomenes of Messenia: 144
Ariston (king): 132
Aristotle's *Lakedaimonion Politeia*: 17-19
Arkhidamos II: 77, 136
Arkhidamos (brother of Agis IV): 20
assembly: 7-8, 45, 66, 133-5, 141
Athenian admirers of Sparta: 15-16
Aulon: 29, 31, 137

bastards: 49, 87
betrothal: 77-81
Brasidas: 29, 41
Brazen-house, precinct of Athena: 136
burial of the dead: 120-2

capital punishment: 144-6
cavalry: 67
celibacy: 73-6
childbirth, woman dying in: 121-2
children, birth and legitimacy: 72-3, 76-7, 83-8
    exposure in infancy: 52-4, 71
    upbringing of boys: 54-65, 152-3

INDEX OF SUBJECTS

upbringing of girls: 71-2
cloak, red: 121
clothes: 45, 55, 164
cook: 118
cowardice: 44-6, 70, 148

Dekhas: 145
Delphic oracle: 3-4
Demaratos (king): 14, 77-8, 81, 86, 134
Derkyllidas: 75-6
desertion, in battle: 70
disfranchisement: 42-6, 58, 70
divorce: 82-3
doctor: 118
dogs: 114
dowry: 81-2
Drakontios: 146-7
drinking: 113-14

eiren: 54-8, 66-8, 159-66
elders: 52-4, *and see* senate
emigration: 115-16
ephebe: 161-7
ephors: 128-32, 154-6, *and passim*
Epitadeus: 5-6, 99-110, 153-4, 156
epitaph: 120-2
Eurysthenes (king): 2, 24
execution: 144-6
 avoided by exile: 147-9
exile: 146-9
exposure of infants: 52-4, 71
extradition: 147

family: 152-4
fighting, among young men: 67-8
fine: 148-50
food: 55-6, 59-61, 111-14
foreigners, communication discouraged: 115, 133
freedman: 39-42, 50-1
funeral: 120-2
furniture: 114

Geranor: 29
gerousia: *see* senate
gold coinage: 5, 9, 118-20, 154, 156
Gylippos: 44, 47-50, 118
gymnastics: 68-9, 71-2
Gymnopaidiai: 75

hair, long: 15, 66, 114, 167
harmost: 11, 13, 29, 148
heiress: 95-7, 107-9
hellanodikai: 124-5, 132-3
helots: 23-5, 31-42, 60
Herakleia: 140
herald: 117-18
Herippidas: 140
hippagretai: 67
Hipponoidas: 148
homicide: 37, 53, 127, 146-7, 151
homosexuality: 61-5, 75
horses: 67, 114
house, construction: 114
 demolished as penalty: 149

illegitimacy: 49, 87
infants: 52-4, 71
inheritance: 94-110, 153-4
investigation by ephors: 137-40
Isadas: 150
Ismenias of Thebes: 133
Ithome, revolt at: 38

jewellery: 114

Kaiadas: 144-6
Kallikratidas: 47-50
Keadas: 144-6
Khilon (son of Demarmenos): 77-8
Kinadon: 31, 117, 127, 131, 137, 149
kings: 123-35, *and passim*
Kleandridas: 44, 49
Kleolas: 138-40
Kleomenes I: 131, 138-41
Kleomenes II: 140
Kleomenes III: 17, 19-20, 34, 48, 73, 99
Kleonymos (son of Kleomenes II): 135
Kritias: 15-16
Kyniska (sister of Agesilaos II): 109
Kythera: 29-30

Lampito (daughter of Leotykhidas II): 77
land, equal lots: 89-99
  held by freedmen: 41-2
  held by helots: 32-4, 41
  held by kings: 28
  held by perioikoi: 28, 91
  held by women: 95-7, 107-9
  inherited: 94-110
  in Messenia: 33-4, 93-4, 98
  reform by Epitadeus: 99-110
  reform proposed by Agis IV: 5, 91
  sale and mortgage: 106-7
legend of Sparta: 14-16
legislative procedure: 5-8
Leobotas (king): 1-2
Leon (king): 2
Leonidas I: 2
Leonidas II: 7
Leotykhidas II: 77-8, 114, 133-4, 148-9
Leotykhidas (reputed son of Agis II): 86, 134, 140
Lepreon: 41-2
leskhe: 53
Leuktra, battle of: 13, 44, 104-5
light, forbidden at night: 68-9
Lykaion: 147
Lykourgos: 1-3, *and passim*
Lykourgos of Athens: 5, 69-70
Lysander: 17, 47-50, 65, 73-4, 118, 124
Lysander (supporter of Agis IV): 6
Lysanoridas: 148

Maiandrios of Samos: 131
Mantineia, battle of (in 418): 148
marriage: 45, 72-88, 152

INDEX OF SUBJECTS

Megalopolis, battle of: 44
Menandros (harmost): 30
mess: 42-3, 49, 60, 69, 111-14
Messenia: 27, 31-5, 93-4, 98
military service, compulsory:
    28, 35, 66, 68
  cowardice and desertion:
    44-6, 70, 116, 126
  exemption: 76
  judgement during campaign:
    124-6, 131
  laws: 69-70
Minyai: 145-6
money-making: 38, 116-18
mortgage: 106-7
mothakes: 46-51, 95
mourning: 120-2
moustache: 155

naturalization: 46-51
neodamodeis: 39-41, 51, 117
nomophylakes: 133
nudity: 71, 75, 150

obedience: 14, 55, 155-6
obes: 26-7
officials, as judges: 123-35
  dismissal by ephors: 131
  eligibility: 45, 66, 167

paidonomos: 55-8, 68
paternal authority: 54, 58, 77-81
patronomoi: 133
Pausanias (king): 131, 141-2,
    144, 147

Pausanias (regent): 137, 144,
    146
penalties: 144-50
  for boys: 57-61
  for helots: 37
  for perioikoi: 31
  sentencing procedure: 142-3
  vicarious: 64
Perikles: 147
perioikoi: 23-5, 27-31, 60-1
Perkalos (daughter of Khilon):
    77-8
Phoibidas: 149-50
Phokion: 49
phratries: 27
Phylarkhos: 19-21
piper: 118
Plataia, battle of: 165
Plataians, defeated in 427: 133
Plato's view of Sparta: 16
Pleistoanax (king): 147-9
Plutarch's sources and
    methods: 17-22
poetry, during campaign: 69-70
polemarchs: 29, 133, 148
Polydoros (king): 4, 90-1, 98
polygamy: 82-8
poverty, causing loss of
    Spartiate status: 49, 112
priests, burial of: 121, 165
prison: 145-6, 149
Prokles (king): 2
prophet: 118
prosecution procedure: 135-41
Pyrrhos: 49

religious cases: 124
retrial: 143-4
rhetra, meaning: 3
    of Epitadeus: 5-6, 99-110, 153-4, 156
    'the Great': 4, 19
    written: 3-5
roads: 123

sale: 45, 106
sanctuary: 147
senate: 6-8, 83, 123, 126-9, 134-5, 139-43
shaving: 45
shopping, not done by young men: 66
silver coinage: 5, 9, 58, 118-20, 154, 156
skytale: 139
slaves: 25, 37-42, 114, 117
Sokrates: 15
Solon: 3
Spartiates: 25-7, *and passim*
speeches at trial: 136-7, 140-1
Sphairos: 19
Sphakteria, men who surrendered at: 44-6
Sphodrias: 141

Tainaron: 38, 137
Tantalos: 29
taxation: 28, 76
Teisamenos of Elis: 50
Theares: 38
theft: 59-61, 151
Thektamenes: 128

Theophrastos, *Laws*: 138
Theopompos (king): 4
Thibron: 148
Thorax: 119, 128
Thouria: 165
three hundred (*corps d'élite*): 66-8
Thyrea: 29
travel abroad: 115-16
trial procedure: 135-44
tribes: 26-7, 52-4
Tyrtaios's poems, recited to army: 69-70

unwritten law: 5

Vatican palimpsest (Vat. Gr. 2306): 138-43
voting at trials: 141-2

whipping: 55, 149
women: 71-88, 95-7, 107-9, 114
work, menial: 116-18
written law: 5-6
written notice of trial: 140
written record of evidence: 139

Xenophon's *Lakedaimonion Politeia*, authenticity and date: 8-14
Xenophon's sons, brought up in Sparta: 49

young men (between twenty and thirty): 66-8, 79, 113, 160-7